Conures

CAROL FRISCHMANN

Conure

Project Team
Editor: Tom Mazorlig
Copy Editor: Stephanie Fornino
Interior Design: Leah Lococo Ltd. and Stephanie Krautheim
Design Layout: Patricia Escabi

T.F.H. Publications
President/CEO: Glen S. Axelrod
Executive Vice President: Mark E. Johnson
Publisher: Christopher T. Reggio
Production Manager: Kathy Bontz

T.F.H. Publications, Inc.
One TFH Plaza
Third and Union Avenues
Neptune City, NJ 07753

Discovery Communications, Inc. Book Development Team
Maureen Smith, Executive Vice President & General
  Manager, Animal Planet
Carol LeBlanc, Vice President, Licensing
Elizabeth Bakacs, Vice President, Creative Services
Peggy Ang, Vice President, Animal Planet Marketing
Caitlin Erb, Licencing Specialist

Printed and bound in China
07 08 09 10 11 1 3 5 7 9 8 6 4 2

Library of Congress Cataloging-in-Publication Data
Frischmann, Carol.
 Conures / Carol Frischmann.
p. cm.
Includes bibliographical references.
ISBN 978-0-7938-3770-0 (alk. paper)
1. Conures. I. Title.
SF473.C65F75 2007
636.6'865–dc22
2006039820

This book has been published with the intent to provide accurate and authoritative information in regard to the sub-
ject matter within. While every precaution has been taken in preparation of this book, the author and publisher
expressly disclaim responsibility for any errors, omissions, or adverse effects arising from the use or application of
the information contained herein. The techniques and suggestions are used at the reader's discretion and are not to
be considered a substitute for veterinary care. If you suspect a medical problem consult your veterinarian.

The Leader In Responsible Animal Care For Over 50 Years!™
www.tfh.com

Table of Contents

Chapter 1

Why I Adore My

Conure

People keep conures as companions because these engaging, playful, gorgeous parrots have the endless capacity to fascinate. Conures' feathers, even the "plain" green ones, glitter like gems. Imitating sounds and human speech, conures tantalize the imagination. Watching them dexterously handle twigs, leaves, and food allows the human companion to envision life in a treetop, surrounded by creatures unlike themselves. And in a world in which life often seems commonplace, who wouldn't want a constant reminder of the extraordinary? Who wouldn't want to touch wild nature?

As alluring as conures are, you have to love the work of giving a companion or pet bird an interesting life. In fact, because conures are so different from humans and from other household pets, especially dogs and cats, this interspecies relationship can be challenging.

Wild, vocal, and adapted for life in the jungle, a conure can stress a family already leading an overcommitted life. Conures also are more work than some other birds, which can add to the stress. Beginners or busy families may want to consider a domesticated bird such as a budgerigar (parakeet) or a cockatiel as a first bird.

The Results of Poor Choices

Not understanding a conure's requirements often results in abandonment. People abandon conures in several ways. Sometimes, "troublesome" conures are placed in a room away from the family, doomed to a dull, unsatisfying life. Conures also are given to friends or relatives, left at shelters, or even set free when they act exactly as a human companion should have expected—as a wild animal with a different set of needs.

Learning as much as possible about the conure will help you to decide

Conures are beautiful, intelligent, and playful, but they are also a big responsibility. A jandaya conure is pictured here.

whether your life has room for this demanding but satisfying pet.

What Is a Conure?

Conures are members of the group of birds called parrots (sometimes called psittacines, pronounced *sit-a-seens*). In the wild, conures live in flocks in Central and South America. In the family home, these birds live as a part of a flock that includes your family members and your other pets. In bringing a conure into your family, you are committing to understanding the conure family and providing for the bird's needs as much as you would for any other member of your family.

Ten Questions to Answer Before Acquiring a Conure

1. Am I purchasing a bird on impulse?
2. Am I willing to pay for an annual exam, proper food, and toys for this bird?
3. Am I willing to spend at least 30 minutes each day interacting with my bird?
4. Can my neighbors, my family, and I live with a conure's normal vocalizations?
5. Will I clean the cage daily?
6. Will I pay for boarding when I go on vacation?
7. Will I forgive bites that result from misunderstandings?
8. Do I understand that I am committing to this pet for 30 years?
9. Will my family help me with my bird?
10. Will I set aside space for the bird that is ideal for him?

Except for the first, your answer to each of these questions should be "yes." If it is not, you should wait to get a conure until you can truthfully answer "yes."

General Characteristics of Conures

Ranging in size from about 8 to 18 inches (20.3 to 45.7 cm) from beak to tip of tail, conures have a slender and light bone structure. The area around a conure's eyes, the eye-ring, is without feathers and usually white. A conure's nostrils are always visible, even if feathered.

Most of these birds are green, with red or another signal color on the wing, under the wings, and on the tail feathers. These contrasting colors provide a dazzling effect in flight and in courtship.

Conures offer the dramatic personality and the coloring of a large parrot, such as a macaw, packed into a smaller body. More available and affordable than larger birds, conures nevertheless require the same commitment of energy and attention that larger parrots do.

Most conures can learn simple tricks such as waving or whistling on command. They love to hang upside down, listen to music, and hang out with their people. Many can learn to talk, and most imitate common household sounds.

Wild

Different from most companion animals, conures are not domesticated. Unlike dogs and cats, who have been bred for thousands of generations to be loyal companions, conures have been bred by humans for only a few generations.

Although conures can make good companions, they are far different from domestic animals. Until they are trained and socialized, these birds make no attempt to please their families. Their language, consisting of postures and calls that most people don't understand, can frustrate their owners.

Lots of learning is required to understand the needs and attitudes of these enchanting animals. For some people, this learning is a fascination, a driving force that keeps them loving the interaction all their lives. For unprepared people, the lack of common understanding and constant demands of this amazing bird result in frustrated, unhappy companions and conures who need new homes.

Conures, such as this sun conure, are only a few generations away from their wild ancestors and retain all their wild instincts.

Vocal
Long before you see a conure, his voice reaches you. Conures' voices evolved to communicate over long distances to flock members in neighboring trees or to keep the group together while in flight. Their vocal range and power intimidate and inspire awe.

Unusual Abilities
A conure's rounded bill is his most prominent characteristic. Curved back toward the body, the bill hinges to the skull. Although it looks rock solid, the bill moves like a hinge, the mobility increasing its power. A conure's powerful bill is useful in opening hard seeds and nuts, for example.

Conures grasp and bring food to their mouths with their feet. Their sensitive tongues, covered in taste buds, manipulate food as well as the human finger can. Conures' toes positioned with two pointing forward and two pointing back (technically, this arrangement is called being *zygodactylus*) to aid in climbing through trees and in manipulating objects, including food.

Temperament and Behavior
Conures and other parrots chatter to each other in the wild and with their human companions because

they are social animals who are most comfortable in flocks. Preferring to perch high in trees, conures will come down to feed and to drink if food and water can't be found in the treetops. Most conures love to bathe in rain, sometimes hanging head down among wet leaves.

Parrots stand still when frightened, silent until the danger passes. Slow and deliberate in walking, climbing, and eating, a conure may raise his foot or hiss when annoyed. Most parrots are left-footed.

To sleep, they gather in flocks, stand on one leg, and hide the other in the belly plumage. When sleeping, the head is usually turned around, hidden in the back plumage.

Most parrots, including conures, nest in hollows in trees. As a result, they have a natural tendency to gnaw wood. They defend small spaces that remind them of nests as they mature, and they will exhibit courtship behaviors to their human companions or to their companions' friends. Like other parrots, conures take a long time to mature. The sexes usually look similar to each other, requiring a DNA test or another conure to tell the sexes apart.

Intelligent and playful, conures can be extremely, eternally entertaining. Given enough space, they can be acrobatic, despite their square bodies. Conures are also active, clownish, water loving, moody, and messy.

A conure's beak is often used as an extra foot when climbing about.

Conure Clans

Scientists divide conures into two main clans (scientifically called a *genus*, plural *genera*) and several smaller ones. The two largest genera are the *Pyrrhura* (pronounced *pir-uhr-rah*) and the *Aratinga* (pronounced *air-uh-tin-guh*).

The word *Pyrrhura* comes from Greek words meaning "red tail." Rosemary Low, noted aviculturist and former curator at Loro Parque Fundación, describes the *Pyrrhura* clan as "quiet-voiced conures with intricate plumage." Attractive and inquisitive birds who originate from Central and South America, the males and females are colored alike. *Pyrrhura* range in size from 9 to 11 inches (22.9 to 27.9 cm), and 9 of the 16 species of *Pyrrhura* are regularly bred in captivity. Small, with moderate voices for parrots, these conures can make excellent pets.

Twenty-one species of conure make up the genus called *Aratinga*, a Tupi Indian name for parrot. *Aratinga* come in sizes ranging from 9 to 14 inches (22.9-35.6 cm). Members of this genus typically have louder, harsher voices than their *Pyrrhura* cousins but share the same characteristic coloring for both male and female birds.

Two conures outside these clans to consider as pets are the Patagonian and Nanday conures.

Fourteen Popular Companion Conures

Some species of conure have several different names, and the spelling of the names vary. The following list includes conures' common names from Thomas Arndt's *Atlas of Conures*. Conures' scientific names are included in italics for enthusiasts who wish to find natural history information on the Internet or in other references. Additional names are included for the reader's convenience.

The color description assumes that the bird's color is green overall unless

Bird Bands

All birds for sale should be banded. A *closed* band, like a bracelet without a clasp, indicates that the bird was bred for the pet trade, rather than wild caught.

Each breeder is registered and has a group of bands for her use. The breeder slips the band over the baby bird's leg. Shortly after the band is slipped over the foot, the bird's foot grows too large for the band to be taken off, except by cutting. The band becomes a permanent record.

These bands were instituted as part of the effort to stop the trapping and selling of wild birds. Birds who were wild caught and sold legally may have a band but not a closed band.

otherwise noted. A conure's potential for speech and other behavior notes are subjective but can be used as general guidelines.

Breeders, companions, scientists, and behaviorists contributed information to this list. The profiles were developed based on species

feather tips and tail dark blue. Orange around eyes and abdomen.
Size: 12 inches (30.5 cm); 5 ounces (141.7 g).
Life expectancy: 25 years.
Potential to talk: Slight talking ability.
Behavior notes: Most commonly kept *Aratinga*. Sociable. Likes to bathe and chew. Does not gnaw as much as the jandaya but requires twigs and toys to destroy.
Natural habitat: Savannah and dry forest with palm groves in northeastern South America.

characteristics. Individual birds may or may not be consistent with the general characteristics of their species.

Golden-Capped Conure
(Aratinga auricapilla)

Colors: Forehead and eyes red-orange; underwing, breast, and abdomen are red-brown. The flight feathers and tail tip are blue.
Size: 12 inches (30.5 cm); 5 ounces (141.7 g).
Life expectancy: 25 years.
Potential to talk: Some talking ability.
Behavior notes: Peaceful but interesting. A frequent, lengthy bather, gnawing urge pronounced.
Natural habitat: Southwestern Brazil along forest edges.

Sun Conure
(Aratinga solstitialis)

Colors: Almost entirely yellow. Flight

Jandaya Conure
(Aratinga jandaya)

Note: This is sometimes called the janday conure or the jenday conure.
Colors: Head and nape yellow-orange; breast and abdomen red; black bill.
Size: 12 inches (30.5 cm); 4 ounces (113.4 g).
Life expectancy: 25 years.
Potential to talk: Can repeat a few words.
Behavior notes: Playful birds who need lots of toys to destroy. Gnaws to the extent that caging should contain no wooden parts. Loves to bathe. Distrustful of new people, objects, and experiences. Loud voices can lead to neighbor troubles.

11

Gold-capped conures are closely related to but less common than sun and jandaya conures.

gnaws minimally. A moderate-voiced bird, even when excited. Stubborn and somewhat rigid about food choices. Spunky, mischievous, and energetic.
Natural habitat: Lowland forests, woodlands, and mossy cloud forests in parts of Brazil, Argentina, and Bolivia.

Blue-Crowned Conure
(Aratinga acuticaudata)

Note: Also called the sharp-tailed conure.
Colors: Forehead, crown of head, and face are blue. Area under the tail brownish red. Upper beak light horn color while lower beak is black. White ring around eye.
Size: 15 inches (38.1 cm); 3 ounces (85 g).
Life expectancy: 30 to 40 years.
Potential to talk: Can learn words; is a good mimic but has a harsh voice.
Behavior notes: Interesting, more easygoing than most conures. Good pet potential.
Natural habitat: Forests in Bolivia, Paraguay, Uruguay, and Argentina.

Nanday Conure
(Nandayus nenday)

Note: This conure is sometimes called the black-hooded conure.
Colors: Dark head and bill, blue flight feathers and breast.
Size: 12 inches (30.5 cm); 4 ounces (113.4 g).

Natural habitat: Woods and scrub of northeast Brazil. Favors coconut palm trees.

Green-Cheeked Conure
(Pyrrhura molinae)

Colors: Forehead and crown brown, throat and upper breast brownish gray, maroon on belly and tail. Primary feathers blue.
Size: 10 inches (25.4 cm); 2 to 3 ounces (56.6 to 85 g).
Life expectancy: 25 years.
Potential to talk: Not likely to talk.
Behavior notes: Lively, bathes regularly,

Life expectancy: 35 to 45 years.
Potential to talk: Good.
Behavior notes: Overall good pet if you can handle loud, frequent squawks and screeches. Flexible, loves showers, likes other birds, needs wood toys.
Natural habitat: Rio Paraguay basin in open country. Prefers palm trees.

Peach-Fronted Conure
(Aratinga aurea)
Colors: Forehead orange; flight feathers and tail tips blue.
Size: 10 inches (25.4 cm); 3 ounces (85 g).
Life expectancy: 25 years.
Potential to talk: Good.
Behavior notes: Strong gnawers, enthusiastic bathers, good at tricks. Not

cuddly. Can be territorial about cage.
Natural habitat: Open low woods of Brazil and Argentina.

Red-Masked Conure
(Aratinga erythrogenys)
Note: Also called the cherry-headed conure.
Colors: Head, lower cheeks, thighs, and underwing are red. Young birds show no red and are often confused with white-eyed conures.
Size: 13 inches (33 cm); 7 ounces (199.4 g).
Life expectancy: 25 years.
Potential to talk: Can learn sentences, excellent mimics of sound.
Behavior notes: Can be very tame.

Enthusiastic bathers with a strong gnawing urge. Loud callers.
Natural habitat: Lowlands of southwest Ecuador and northwest Peru.

Patagonian Conure
(Cyanoliseus patagonus)
Colors: Olive-brown appearance with yellow belly and red center patch. Blue flight feathers and white eye ring.
Size: 17 inches (44 cm);

The Expert Knows

It's All Relative

Conure's names, like the scientific names for Patagonian, sun, and jandaya conures, are assigned based on what we know about the relationships of parrot species. New research techniques allow investigators to examine parrot DNA to understand more about how conures are really related to one another and to other parrots. Recently published scientific papers about sections of DNA from *Aratinga* conures suggest that the conure family tree may again be redrawn. Stay tuned for further discoveries based on advances in science as researchers take our knowledge of parrot relationships to a new level.

Green-cheeked conures are one of the quieter conures, but they still can be loud when the mood strikes them.

8 to 11 ounces (240 to 310 g).
Life expectancy: 30 years or more.
Potential to talk: Good.
Behavior notes: Social, touchable, playful birds. Enthusiastic bathers. Gnawing urge strong. Prefer the ground rather than perches for feeding and play.
Natural habitat: Open grassy lowlands in Argentina, Uruguay, and Chile.

Orange-Fronted Conure
(Aratinga canicularis)
Note: Also called the half-moon conure, because the orange band across the forehead is shaped like a half-moon.
Colors: Orange-red band across forehead, blue crown and flight feathers.

Size: 10 inches (25.4 cm); 3 ounces (85 g).
Life expectancy: 25 years.
Potential to talk: Good mimics.
Behavior notes: One of the smallest Aratingas. Demands time with people and can learn tricks but doesn't care to snuggle. Gnawing urge is minor.
Natural habitat: Lightly treed lowlands from northwestern Mexico to northwestern Costa Rica.

Green Conure
(Aratinga holochlora)
Colors: Pale green under wing and white eye ring.
Size: 12 inches (30.5 cm); 8.2 oz. (232g)
Life expectancy: 25 years.
Potential to talk: Not known to talk. Have a loud voice.
Behavior notes: Gnawers, enthusiastic bathers, sociable.
Natural habitat: Lowland woods from Nicaragua to Texas border.

White-Eyed Conure
(Aratinga leucophthalmus)
Colors: Red feathering on head, neck, underwing edge, and thighs. Yellow underwing.
Size: 12 inches (30.5 cm); 5 ounces (141.7 g)
Life expectancy: 30 years or more.
Potential to talk: Can imitate some words; good mimic of sounds.

Behavior notes: Quick, shy bird with great pet potential for a sensitive keeper. Heavy gnawers. Loves baths and is curious and clownish.
Natural habitat: Throughout South America in lowland forests and woodlands.

Dusky-Headed Conure
(Aratinga weddellii)
Note: Also called Weddell's conure.
Colors: Head is gray-brown with blue feather tips. Primary flight feathers are black with blue edges, and the tail is blue. Eye ring is white.
Size: 10 inches (25.4 cm); 3 ounces (85 g).
Life expectancy: 25 years.
Potential to talk: Not a great mimic.
Behavior notes: Shy with a strong gnawing need. Uniquely quiet among *Aratinga*, dusky-headeds will hardly ever utter the conure's high piercing sound.

Wild Parrots of Telegraph Hill

Mark Bittner's relationship with a feral flock of conures, including many red-masked conures, is chronicled in the book and film, *The Wild Parrots of Telegraph Hill.* The film, available on DVD, gives the viewer an idea of the vocal range of conures and highlights their intelligence and social interactions.

Expresses self by chirping and purring. Loves to cuddle. A calm and steady bird.
Natural habitat: Brazil's Amazon Basin lowland forest.

Black-Capped Conure
(Pyrrhura rupicola)
Note: Also called the rock conure. There is a subspecies, *Pyrrhura rupicola sandiae*, that is called the Sandia conure.
Colors: Forehead, crown, nape, and throat are brown; edge of wing and wing feathers red.
Size: 10 inches (25.4 cm); 2.6 oz (75g)
Life expectancy: 25 years.
Potential to talk: Limited.
Behavior notes: Lively but timid. Good bathers and enthusiastic gnawers. They have subdued voices and are not choosy eaters.

Peach-fronted conures tend to be good at talking and mimicry.

The orange-fronted conure is also called the half-moon conure.

Natural habitat: Lowland tropical forests in central Peru.

Selecting a Pet Conure

If you decide that you want a conure in your life, the selection process involves several decisions. The type of conure is one decision. Another is the age of the bird. A final consideration is the individual bird.

The conure group includes 48 species (further divided into 72 subspecies). The number of species makes the choice sound complicated, but we will simplify the process by considering only those conures who are most readily available as pets.

Set Your Criteria in Advance

You wouldn't go to the grocery store without a list or at least an idea in mind of what you needed for the household. With conures, if you choose one before you decide your own limits, you may bring home a bird who doesn't suit your lifestyle.

Questions that breeders are most often asked are about talking ability, color, and the "cuddly" factor, but other vital criteria to consider include your living circumstances (country versus apartment with thin walls), your ability to live with noise and mess, your level of patience, and your willingness to spend time with

Dusky-headed conures generally are quiet conures that love to cuddle with their companions.

FAMILY-FRIENDLY TIP

A Conure as a Child's Pet

Whether a conure is a good choice of pet for a child depends on the individual child, the home situation, and the individual animal. Pets help children learn empathy toward others, especially when parents ask questions that help their children to understand the animal. Another benefit is an increase in self-esteem when children are praised for accomplishing pet care tasks. Success depends on the parent knowing what tasks are age appropriate. Below is a table to help you make those decisions, but you must remember that every child and every conure is an individual.

Child's Age	Suggestions for Parents	Cautions
up to 2	Keep conure secured.	Keep pet from soiled diapers.
3–4	Demonstrate care, reinforce child's petting or helping with care, and incorporate bird in play.	Make sure child washes hands and doesn't feed conure innappropriate items. Supervise play.
5-10	Remind child to feed conure and clean cage.	Make sure child washes hands. Supervise play.
11+	Oversee child's care of pet	Parental oversight necessary.

your bird. Finally, you'll want to know about the special characteristics of a species, such as the need to gnaw or the tendency to vocalize. You'll have a conure for a long time, so you need to know what you're committing to.

Sources of Conures

You've completed your list of requirements. You have impressions about the type of conure whom you'd like to have as a companion. The next step is meeting some conures.

As you look at the conures, keep your list of requirements and questions in mind. Best is a situation where you can visit several sources of the birds and take a few days to consider what you've seen. Conures last longer than many marriages, so be selective.

Pet Stores

Large chain pet stores often sell birds, including some of the more frequently seen conures. If you have other pets, you've probably seen the birds when you came in to pick up pet food.

Another possibility is a store that specializes in selling pet birds and supplies. There are usually one or two stores in a major metro area. The more specialized store will tend to have a staff that is more knowledgeable about your particular type of bird, and the staff is more likely to have time to work with you and your prospective bird.

When purchasing from any pet store, health is a consideration because birds may come from many different suppliers. As the group of birds enlarges and the number of suppliers increases, the potential for diseases expands, too. Most pet stores will guarantee the health of the birds they are selling. If you find a store that won't do this, you should look elsewhere for your companion.

Breeders

Another alternative is to buy directly from a breeder. In most cases, breeders are excellent sources of healthy birds. Most breeders will spend a good deal of time educating you about your new

Considerations in Purchasing a Conure

1. Decide whether you have the desire necessary to care for a lifetime companion.
2. Make a list of ideal characteristics for your companion.
3. Study profiles of various conure choices.
4. Eliminate birds who do not meet the list of desired characteristics.
5. Visit sources of conures and ask questions.
6. Select one or two types to consider in depth.
7. Consider the age, sex, health, and history of the available birds.
8. Spend time with individuals who meet your criteria.
9. Take a week to think it over.
10. Visit again.
11. Purchase with a health certificate or guarantee.
12. Take conure for veterinary examination.
13. Final purchase of conure.

conure's needs and will be available to answer questions as you bring your new companion into the family. Breeders can be found through the American Federation of Aviculture (www.afabirds.org) and the International Conure Association (www.conure.org).

Humane Organizations

Shelters or rescue organizations are other sources of birds. Most humane societies have birds for adoption, as do bird rescue organizations and exotic bird clubs. Keep in mind, however, that a foster and rescue network serves the increasing number of birds given up by the people who purchased them. Knowing the reason that your potential companion was surrendered is important. Owners who made poor choices in pet selection may be surrendering birds with behavior or diet-related health problems.

Age

Birds of all ages are available, from the newly weaned to the senior bird. Because the life expectancy of conures in good health is substantial, age should be a major consideration.

Mature birds provide many advantages, including the fact that their personalities are fully formed, their coloration is developed, and their habits are well established. In other words, you have a realistic glimpse of your lives together from the beginning. Conures over the age of two are mature. Birds over the age of 12 to 25, depending on species, are seniors.

Newly weaned or young conures offer a completely different experience. If you choose one of these birds, you will have

Although not the most colorful of conures, Patagonian conures make wonderful pets.

One Bird or Two?

Unless you have an extraordinary amount of time or more space than most people can devote to their conure, you should begin with one bird. Building a relationship with a bird takes time, and these days, time is one thing that most people don't have enough of.

Many people believe that birds need a second bird to be happy, but that isn't necessarily true. Companion birds see you as their flock. Another bird may only complicate the situation.

In addition, until you are confident in your abilities to handle your conure and to deal with the noise and the mess, you'll be glad you have just one bird companion.

the pleasure of watching your bird mature and the pain of watching much of his sweetness disappear into a more staid and likely less tolerant companion.

Feathers acquire their adult coloration in a process that lasts at least one year and sometimes more. Another aspect of maturation is the behavioral changes. As the young of any species go through developmental stages, so do conures. Generally, the longer lived the species, the longer the developmental stages.

One caution: A mature conure will

not retain all the baby-like qualities of the immature conure. Adult conures are as different from baby conures as parents are from their small children. Get to know an adult of the species or maybe several adults before choosing a youngster.

Health

The best indicator of health is general appearance, and at the "just looking" stage, that's what you should rely on. What to look for? A healthy bird has clear eyes and cere (the strip where skull and beak meet, containing the nostrils), smooth feathers, all his toes, and clean legs and feet. His vent (where the bird eliminates feces) will be clean. The conure will be active in his cage, show curiosity, and perhaps approach you. If you're not sure whether a bird is healthy, move on.

Birds who are molting can provide a confusing experience if you're not accustomed to seeing them develop feathers. The developing feather pokes through the skin from the inside, and the feather emerges covered with a coating made of a material similar to a human cuticle. This is normal, although young birds look slightly alien covered in these developing feathers.

Older birds replace all their feathers once each year and molt to replace individual feathers year round. The spiky-coated feathers sometimes cause people to assume that the bird is ill, but this is not the case.

Another indicator of health is the appearance of the enclosure in which the bird has been kept. The cage should not show a buildup of feces or dried food. The water should be clean. The room should be light and relatively clean. Birds are messy, but the facility should give the appearance of having been cleaned daily. The birds' food and water should appear to have been changed twice daily.

History

You probably want a bird who has been handled from an early age because they are already socialized. Buying directly from a breeder helps you to find a bird who has been handled consistently from early on in his life. There is great variation in how often birds are handled at different stores. Bird-only stores generally do the best job of ensuring that their birds are handled daily.

A mishandled conure's reactions will not change immediately with placement in a loving home. Resolving these problems is something that a first-time conure companion should not attempt, because it takes skill and patience. In fact, love will not be enough to solve the behavior problems. Unfortunately, some problems may never be overcome sufficiently to transform a bird into a satisfying companion, even in the hands of a professional trainer.

Knowing a bird's history is especially important if you wish to choose a bird from a rescue organization. Often, these birds are in these situations because the original family did not know or did not try to provide what they needed. As a result, rescued conures may be fearful or have bad habits that are difficult for the novice bird keeper to overcome.

The Expert Knows

Selecting Talkers

Whether your bird talks or not is more a function of the species of bird and the environment, rather than the sex. While it appears in some kinds of birds that males talk more frequently than females, conure males and females are equally talkers or nontalkers. From the profile list, the pet conure species best known for talking include blue-crowned, nanday, orange-fronted, Patagonian, peach-fronted, and red-masked conures.

Considering the Senior Conure

Consider adopting a senior conure. Birds usually enter into shelters for one of two reasons: behavior problems or changes in a person's life circumstances. Some very nice companion conures enter shelters because their human companions passed away. Senior birds have established personalities and needs, and many who enter shelters for this reason are well mannered.

Your commitment to your new conure is for the rest of his life. In the case of a senior conure, his lifetime is not the 30 years that you can expect from a youngster.

If you want to adopt a shelter bird, talk to the organization's bird keepers or the foster family. Tell them that you are a first-time bird owner, that you have experience with parakeets and cockatiels, or whatever your experience truly is. Some perfectly lovely birds who are suitable for advanced bird handlers are a nightmare for first-time owners. You wouldn't enter a marathon in your first month of running. Don't try a wild-caught or problem bird without training either. Leave those birds to the experienced. You and the bird will be much happier.

A Good Approach to Familiarization and Purchase

Once you've identified several potential birds, look at each of them a second time. Spend time with several birds in an environment that mimics your home. Take a book like this one

This black-capped conure is enjoying a healthy treat.

Life Expectancy

Conures vary in their life expectancy, from 15 years to 45 years. If you join forces with a conure when you're 25, you may have the conure until you are 70, nearly all your adult life.

If you select a conure when you're 12, you could be 57 at the end of his life. At that time, you might have grandchildren who are 12. Imagine a pet whom you've known longer than your mate or your children!

and read it carefully. Bathe the bird or feed him. Observe how the facility's staff handles him.

Discuss the purchasing process. What paperwork does the seller provide? You should expect to receive:

- a bill of sale that provides a description of the bird, the sale price, and the hatch date and band number of the bird
- a care sheet that describes the routine of the bird

- a health guarantee for the bird that explains the right of return

If your prospective seller is unwilling to provide these things, move on, no matter how much you like the bird. An unwillingness to provide them indicates that the seller is not reliable.

If your prospective seller provides these things, you should return at least once to spend time with the bird you like most. Again, ask to help in his care. Watch the process of caring for your prospective bird and other birds. Talk with the seller about suitable veterinary care in the area, a local bird club, and other resources that may support you in your efforts to become knowledgeable about your companion.

Health Check

Ensure that the bird passes the veterinary examination. You can consider this examination to be the "health test" and also his first annual health examination.

Why all this emphasis on health? Your conure is a substantial investment of your time and emotional energy. In addition, your investment in the purchase of your bird, annual medical care, and proper housing, including toys, is substantial. Ensuring that you have a healthy bird from the beginning means that you are unlikely to have to make even larger investments providing medical support to a bird that was unhealthy from the start.

Chapter 2

The Stuff of

Everyday Life

The stuff of everyday life makes or breaks a relationship. Adding a companion conure is as much a change as adding a roommate—and this roommate is of an unfamiliar species! This means that you're not going to get everything right the first time, but learning about your new companion is going to be half the fun. You may need help, but rest assured, you won't have to do this on your own. Your teachers, in addition to your bird, include everyone you meet in your process of considering a conure.

A good opportunity to learn how to care for your conure is to notice how each shop, breeder, or rescue organization cares for their birds. One keeper may have a great cage arrangement. Another may be a master at food and supply organization. Yet another may have a list of three great avian veterinarians.

After several visits, you'll have clear ideas about how you want to care for your bird. Planning and shopping for the gear that creates a good environment for your conure builds a solid foundation for the long-term happiness that you and your bird deserve.

Purchasing a Cage

In selecting the right cage, place your bird's comfort and your ease of cleaning above aesthetics. Your conure spends most of each day inside his cage. The right choice will repay you and your bird seven times each week—each time that you clean the cage. A beautiful cage can be destructive to your relationship if your bird hates being in it and you hate cleaning it.

During your visits to stores, breeders, and humane organizations, take a close look at the variety of cages. Notice cage size and shape, the distance between the bars, and the variety of cage materials. Study the size and placement of cage doors and food dishes. Ask bird caretakers about their experience with the different cage styles. Which are easiest to clean? Which do their conures prefer? What would they change about the best cages that they have? Although their priorities may not be the same as yours, you will learn a lot from professionals who spend their days with cages and birds. Their information will save you uncertainty and the cost of buying a poorly suited cage, only to find that you must purchase a more suitable one.

What Size?

This cage is the boundary of your bird's universe, except when you take

The size of the cage and the spacing of the bars are just two factors to consider when buying one for your conure.

him out during cleaning or for playtime. Thinking of his cage this way underscores the need that your conure has for the largest cage you can afford. Minimum cage size depends on your bird's size. A cage that works well for a palm-sized conure will not work well for a conure who is longer than your forearm.

Most pet owners compromise when choosing a cage. They select an enclosure that is large enough for the bird to thrive when given plenty of time out of the cage on a play stand but that comfortably fits the human companion's home and budget.

Sleeping Cages

Another way to provide a more varied universe for your bird is to use a separate sleeping cage. Sleeping cages allow your companion to "go to roost" at night, just as he would in the wild. Especially if your conure's cage is in a location that is busy until late in the day, he will benefit from a sleeping cage in a secluded room. Each morning, you accompany your companion as he "leaves the roost" to forage in his day cage.

While not absolutely necessary, a sleeping cage is ideal. (A sleeping cage should be smaller than the day cage but large enough for a stretch without your companion brushing his feathers on the bars.) With clever selection,

Conure Size and Cage Bar Spacing

Size	Species	Length (cm)	Length (in.)	Similar-size Familiar Bird	Smallest Cage Size (in.)	Bar Spacing (in.)
Small	Half-moon	24	9	Robin	20x20	1/2 to 5/8
	Black-capped	25	10			
	Green-cheeked	26	10			
	Peach-fronted	26	10			
	Dusky	28	11			
Medium	Golden-capped	30	12	Flicker	24x24	1/2 to 5/8
	Green	30	12			
	Jandaya	30	12			
	Nanday	30	12			
	Sun	30	12			
	White-eyed	32	13			
	Red-masked	33	13			
Large	Blue-crowned	33	13	American Crow	30x30	5/8 to 3/4
	Patagonian	44	17			

the sleeping cage also can be used as a transport cage for trips to the veterinarian or for short excursions outside.

Cage Shape

Choose a square or rectangular cage instead of a round one. Birds climb and rest more easily in a cage with straight sides. In addition, most manufacturers design accessories such as food dishes, perches, and toys to fit straight-sided cages.

Although pet suppliers make most cages taller than they are wide, most birds use the width of the cage rather than the height. For safety, birds perch at the highest point available. In his enclosure, your conure will spend most of his time on the highest perch. An oblong-shaped cage provides more usable space arranged as the bird prefers. Place the cage atop a cabinet with plenty of storage for supplies, and you have a conure condo that works well for both of you.

Play Tops

Some manufacturers offer a cage-top play area as an option. Play areas provide a perch, toy hangers, and space to climb. They offer a convenient place for your bird to perch while you work inside the cage or for your bird to romp on during supervised playtime.

One caution about cage-top play spaces: You must be able to reach the entire play area to remove the bird.

Play Stands: Alternative to Play Tops

If you find the right cage that does not have a play top, an alternative is a separate play stand. One disadvantage is that you will have two areas to clean, but the advantages are the variety for your bird and the enforced time away from his cage. Birds who do not spend enough time away from their cage often become difficult to handle because they vigorously defend their cage as their only home territory.

Otherwise, he will learn to retreat to the one place you cannot reach. This fabulous game of catch for your bird will be a tiresome journey to retrieve a stepstool each time that you need to cage your playful companion. If your cage is too tall for a play top, you can purchase or create a separate play area that serves your bird's needs.

Wheels

Wheels make moving the cage quick, easy work. Cage cleaning requires wiping the bars inside and out and vacuuming underneath. If you're cleaning the cage daily—and you should—you'll appreciate this feature.

Cage Bar Spacing

Bar spacing is proper when a bird cannot fit his head through the bars.

If his head can pass through, the rest of the bird can follow. Worse, he can wedge his head through too wide bars, panic, and be unable to free himself.

A less obvious problem is bar spacing that narrows toward the top of a cage or is inconsistent due to cage decoration. A bird can pass his head or leg through the bars at their broadest span and climb until the narrow placement does not allow him to withdraw his head or foot. Panic results in injury when your bird realizes that he is trapped and cannot free himself.

Recommended bar spacing for most conures is 1/2 to 3/4 of an inch (1.3 to 1.9 cm). Because of species and individual bird size variations, measure the width of your bird's head to be sure that he can't get it through the bars.

Cage bar arrangement affects how easily your bird can make use of the space inside his cage. Horizontal bars offer more climbing surface, making the entire cage more attractive. Some newer cage designs have reversed the older, less desirable design and made the majority of the bars horizontal and the minority of the bars vertical.

Cage Materials

Wire mesh, powder-coated wire or metal bars, and stainless steel bars are common cage materials. Wire mesh is the least expensive material, and stainless steel is the most expensive.

Wire Mesh Cages

Often used in outdoor aviaries and in a few indoor cages, wire mesh protects your bird from intruders and confines him. Neither mice nor small children's fingers can penetrate the mesh. Mesh

Play tops provide a safe area for your conure to have out-of-cage fun time.

disadvantages include the lack of accessories made for this style of cage and the less attractive appearance for indoor use.

Powder-Coated Cages

A powder-coated cage of wire or metal bars is very durable and easy to clean. A wide variety of accessories is manufactured to fit this type of cage. However, the bar spacing that makes climbing a snap for your bird also allows tiny fingers to penetrate the cage, a disadvantage for a family with toddlers. Although large powder-coated cages can be expensive, they last for many years. People who provide these cages usually report many happy years with design, features, and durability.

Stainless Steel Cages

Stainless steel is the ultimate in cage materials. It looks elegant and lasts almost forever, making this the most desirable—but most expensive—cage.

Wooden Cages

Wooden cages or cages with wooden parts are impossible to sanitize. Worse, they are vulnerable to the persistently gnawing conure. If you think you can stay one step ahead of your bird, think again. In a matter of hours, he will whittle his way to freedom. Forget wooden enclosures for the companion bird. The risk is not worth it.

Acrylic Cages

Acrylic is relatively new as a cage material. Some cages

Keeping the Home-Alone Bird Happy

While you're out during the day, your conure is at home. You want him to be busy. Think about your bird's five senses:

- Sight: Give your bird something interesting to watch—a television, a bird feeder, an aquarium.
- Hearing: Six CDs on random play give a whole day of varied listening pleasure, as does a radio station. Conures love to chatter and whistle at media of all sorts.
- Smell: Conures don't have a great sense of smell, but you might leave a little citrus and mint for your bird to chew. You'll appreciate the fresh fragrance when you return.
- Taste: Make sure that the food is varied and that there's work involved in getting the food. Try food in treat dispensers, delicious leaves hung from the cage top, and fruit on skewers that he has to stretch to reach.
- Touch: Use toys and perches of different textures. Rotating your bird's toys is helpful. Divide your toy stock in half and switch toy sets once a week. Old toys become new when you switch the first set for the second set.

are all acrylic, and some have acrylic front and back panels, the side panels being barred. Although keepers make clever use of the acrylic totes as feeding or sleeping cages, the acrylic cage is not a suitable full-time cage for parrots, especially those who spend long hours each day caged.

In addition, acrylic cages are not a good idea because the material provides no climbing surface and separates your companion from his flock—you. If this material seems irresistible because of the mess containment, you should rethink whether you can tolerate the mess made by a companion bird.

Braided rope perches are also a good choice, as long as you snip off any frayed bits. A sun conure and a painted conure are shown here.

Cage Finish Caution

If you hear the words "lacquer" or "zinc" in the cage description, move on to another option. Galvanized materials, including wire mesh, are unsuitable for birdcages. Although galvanizing prevents rusting, the process uses zinc, which is poisonous to birds.

Cage Grates and Slide-Out Trays

Most cages come with a grate and a slide-out tray, making it simple to remove the bedding material you've chosen to catch droppings. Grates prevent a bird from walking through fouled food or droppings. They also keep your bird caged when you slide out the tray to change the bedding.

Despite the convenient aspects of a grate, keepers who clean their birds' cages daily usually find the grate to be a nuisance because droppings fall on it, creating another surface to clean. If you purchase a cage with a removable grate, you have the option of deciding whether to use it or not.

If you find the perfect cage with the exception that the grate is not removable, consider putting newspaper on top of the grate instead of below, in the pull-out tray. Droppings will fall onto the paper, leaving the grate clean.

Latches and Doors

Confinement, convenience, and cleaning are watchwords for ideal placement and style of latches and doors. Most important is that your conure cannot open the latch. Some birds are so clever at opening latches that you'd swear they had engineering degrees. Either the latch must be heavy or stiff enough that your conure cannot open it or must be out of reach of an inquisitive beak.

Using extreme measures to make poorly constructed latches secure creates a safety problem. For example, a lock or a plastic zip tie can secure any latch. The problem comes when an emergency occurs and you can't get the door open. A latch that your bird can't open but you can open quickly is a basic a requirement for a cage.

Some conures appreciate the comedy of a well-flung bowl and the distress of their human companion afterward, so a feeding bowl compartment that locks your bird's bowl in place may be a welcome feature. This design has the added advantage that people who aren't comfortable handling your bird can provide clean food and water without stressing themselves or the bird. You'll appreciate this when your regular bird-sitter is out of town and your friend, terrified of birds, volunteers to feed if she doesn't have to touch him.

A few cages, especially ones built for smaller birds, use "guillotine-style" doors

A cage with slide-out tray in the bottom is easier to clean than one lacking this feature.

that open and close by sliding up and down. The disadvantage to these doors is that larger birds housed inside make a game of pulling the doors up and letting them fall down. Many birds delight in the power and the bang when the door slams down. Unfortunately, injury can result either from the door crushing the bird or from the events following his escape.

Cage doors should swing out, leaving a gap at least two times the width of the bird on your hand. Less clearance is an invitation for him to grab the bars and refuse to exit his cage. This habit is difficult to break, especially when the cage design encourages it. Cage doors positioned in the middle of the cage allow the human companion to reach all parts of the cage for cleaning.

Seed Skirts

Seed skirts are usually sloping metal strips around the cage's perimeter that direct seed hulls and casual debris back into the cage. Many cages either offer seed skirts as a removable feature or integrate them into the cage's design. The advantage of the skirts is that they keep the area surrounding the cage more debris free. The disadvantage is that they increase the space needed for your cage and create another surface to clean. Some keepers believe it is easier to use a shop vacuum to clean the floors around the cage than it is to clean the seed skirt.

Cage Placement

Cage placement is a strategic decision. This sounds funny, but it's true. Often, cage placement is the difference between a secure and happy bird and one who develops behavior problems. Because your bird will spend most of his life in his cage, the best placement needs to be the priority.

Three characteristics of bird biology are important to consider in cage placement. First, birds are prey animals. Second, a bird's breathing is sensitive to fumes and vapors, drafts, and excessive heat. Finally, birds are social

Bird-Proofing the Home

Homes are not natural environments for birds, just as treetops are not natural for people. We each need help in exploring these different worlds.

Restricting access to creatures and things that will cause curious conures harm is important to your happy life together. Imagine that you were the size of a tennis ball, could fly, had a compulsion to explore everything, and also had the judgment of a two-year-old child. That's your conure. You have to make the assessment for him.

Your bird's cage and play gyms are safe rooms. When he leaves those areas, you must supervise him. You need a family policy about opening doors and windows, indoor cooking, and leaving water exposed.

Common points to check include:

• Open toilet lids and sinks that contain water are drowning hazards.

• Cord from blinds and curtains can entangle birds, causing them to panic.

• Hot stoves, ovens, and woodstoves can burn conures.

• Bric-a-brac on shelves can attract a curious parrot, who might pull an item over on himself.

• Houseplants attract inquisitive birds. Be sure that plants are nontoxic and are not treated with insecticides or fertilizers.

• Craft supplies can be choking hazards, and a conure may think they are toys.

animals who need to be with their human companions

Birds Are Prey Animals

Because he is only one or two generations from the wild, your conure is constantly on the lookout for bird-eating snakes, hawks, and monkeys. This is why sudden movement and unfamiliar sights (hats, new toys, and furniture rearrangement, for example) startle him. In the natural environment, attack could come from any direction. Parrots' vision accommodates this. Notice the placement of their eyes on the side of their heads. With only 6 to 10 percent binocular vision, conures can see everything except what's directly behind them. Their flexible neck allows them to see the rest.

Each time a conure is startled, adrenalin pulses through his body. Adrenalin takes a long time to leave the system, and a constant adrenalin flow is not healthy for any creature. A conure who is frequently startled or who just doesn't feel safe will be constantly secreting adrenalin, and consequently, his health will suffer.

Placing the cage with one long side against a wall helps your bird to experience significantly less stress. Better, choose a corner that protects him on two sides but allows him to see everything going on with the family. If it is on wheels, moving the cage out for cleaning is a snap.

Checklist for Daily Cage Maintenance

- Wipe the cage bars to remove food and feces.
- Remove the soiled paper and replace it with clean paper. As you do this, check to ensure that the droppings look normal.
- Remove the food and water dishes and install clean dishes with fresh food and water. Wipe down obvious trouble spots on toys, checking for loose threads, loose toy hangers, broken edges, and anything else that might harm your bird during the day.
- Check to be sure that all cage doors are latched and that ventilation is adequate for that day's weather.
- Vacuum the surrounding counter and floor.
- Clean up dishes and dispose of trash.

Birds Have Sensitive Respiratory Systems

Remember the stories about the canaries in the mines? Miners took

Your conure will feel most secure if one or two sides of his cage are facing walls.

which the bird evolved—including spray air cleaners and even plug-in air fresheners—are suspect.

Cigarette smoke is bad for you, but it is worse for your bird. For each breath that your bird takes, smoke passes through the lungs twice, once on the way to the air sacs and once on the way back. Also, your bird becomes addicted to nicotine from exposure to your smoke. A final point is that nicotine residue on smokers' hands is transferred to your bird's feathers and feet. When your conure preens, he then ingests the nicotine by mouth. Both smoke and nicotine effects are a serious problem for your conure.

caged canaries into the mine shafts with them. If the canary died, the miners ran for the surface. They knew that the canary was far more sensitive to toxic gases than human beings. Keep in mind, then, that odors that you barely notice can be difficult or deadly for your bird. Cage placement makes a big difference in the exposure your bird may have to these dangers.

Fumes and Vapors

The common source of fumes and vapors is the kitchen. Similarly, work areas such as garages, woodworking shops, and artists' studios can be filled with fumes that, while mildly annoying for people, can be fatal for birds. These areas are not appropriate for your bird's cage.

Anything that creates an aerosol that is not normal to the habitat in

Drafts and Ducts

An indoor bird needs to be free from extremes of heat and cold. Because a cage keeps your conure from escaping an uncomfortable or even dangerous temperature, your placement of the cage needs to anticipate this. Sources of heat and cold include drafts from windows and doors and ducts from your home's central heating and cooling system.

Windows

Windows can be entertainment features for your bird, especially if you place a wild bird feeder outside in his view. However, windows also can be sources of unrelenting heat. Think of how your car heats up in the sun. If you're considering placement near a window, keep a thermometer in that location, even on days that seem cool to you. It doesn't have to be hot outside to create very high temperatures just inside the glass. Thermometers that save the maximum and minimum daily temperatures work for this purpose and are inexpensive. You can get them from carriers of reptile supplies. Use of blinds or shades inside or on awnings outside can reduce temperatures on hot days.

Birds Are Social Animals

Your bird wants to be with you. You are purchasing a companion bird, and he expects you to hold up your end of the bargain. There are two kinds of attention. First, there is direct attention, where you take your bird from the cage and focus on him exclusively. Then there's ambient attention, which means you're hanging out, each doing your own thing but acknowledging each other's presence, maybe talking back and forth or singing a song together. Both kinds of attention are healthy for you and for your bird.

A properly placed cage promotes this type of attention. With your bird's cage placed in a family room that's open to the kitchen, you can talk while you cook. Your children can play with their pet bird while they watch a favorite television program.

A bedroom, on the other hand, is not a good choice for cage location. When you're there, you're sleeping. While you're cooking and hanging out downstairs or down the hall, the bird will call for your attention. He can hear you. He wants to see you. A spare bedroom is an even worse choice. He has the room all to himself, but he doesn't want it. He's a flock animal!

Look at the flow of your house. Your conure's day cage needs to where he can see and respond to you and where you can respond to him while you're awake. His night cage, if you have one, could be in a bedroom. A bird needs 12 hours of uninterrupted quiet each night. You can and should cover your bird's cage at night, but if you're dancing to rap music in your bedroom, he is going to be singing along and be tired and cranky the next day.

For cage placement, think safety first, your bird's need for society second, and your decorating pride third.

Food and Water Bowls

The major points about choosing food and water bowls are that they should be easy to sanitize, that you have several sets to speed your morning and evening routines, and that they are safe for your unsupervised bird. Even if your cage comes with bowls, you may wish to consider other types for reasons of sanitation or variety.

Many larger cages have built-in bowl holders. Some smaller cages, especially those with guillotine doors, come with dishes that fit into the feeder doors. In either case, you need not feel constrained by this. Be sure to get bowls that lock onto the bars rather than those that simply rest on unsecured hooks over the bars. Locking bowls work especially well for birds who consistently upset their bowls.

For your bird, water serves two purposes: drinking and bathing. Many people use a heavy, shallow dish of water on the cage floor for bathing and supply a secured, closed water bottle to dispense clean drinking water. Most birds easily learn to drink from these bottles. While plastic water bottle dispensers work, glass bottles with a substantial rubber stopper and stainless steel spout that affix to the outside of the cage are easier to clean and disinfect, and they last longer, too.

Food and water bowls need to be washed in hot water and replenished daily. Animal professionals prefer to disinfect with a dilute

Conures and Other Pets

Conures mixing with other pets can be complicated. The size difference isn't the only risk factor. Cats and dogs are hunters; birds are prey species. Even when birds are physically separated from cats and dogs, the stress of remaining watchful can create health and behavior problems for your bird.

If you choose not to keep your pets physically separated, the danger increases. Many people do not realize that bacteria in cat saliva may cause infection and death of your pet bird if not treated. Also, puncture wounds are hard to see. If your cat mouths your bird, assume the worst and have him examined immediately.

Dogs usually cruise birdcages because of the constant presence of your conure's food. Some bored parrots even lure dogs by tossing food to them. The natural temperaments of cats, dogs, and birds keep your conure at a disadvantage and under stress without separation. Although conures usually will come to see the dog as harmless, it's best not to let them interact with each other.

A conure can get along with other parrots, but you should supervise them the entire time that they are together. Watch for any signs of aggression between the two parrots, and intervene when necessary. Be especially careful if the birds are of largely different sizes. If you have pets other than dogs, cats, or parrots, allowing them to interact with your conure is a bad idea. Ferrets, for example, are predators and will try to kill birds. Other small mammals can bite your parrot or vice versa. Reptiles are similarly problematic. Your conure will be most content to spend time with you and the other human members of the flock.

bleach solution (10 percent bleach in water) or in a dishwasher with a high temperature setting.

Toys

The right selection of toys will keep your bird busy, challenged, and excited about life when you are not available for play and interaction. The variety of toys available is staggering, so most new companions need a few tips to sort through and select the toys that will work best for conures. The rule of thumb is safety first and variety second.

How do you learn to choose the right toys? Suppliers sometimes tag their toys as appropriate for conures to help new human companions. In addition, stores or online suppliers that specialize in birds can offer personalized advice. A good breeder, bird club, or magazine also can help teach you what you need to know.

To ensure a good variety of toy types, consider placing one or two of each of these types in your bird's normal cage setup: thinking toys, action toys, comfort toys, and toys to destroy. Once you choose the toys, rotate them. Use half the toys one week, and then exchange the toys for the other half of the toy set the following week.

Thinking Toys
Toys that intrigue your bird and

stimulate his mind keep him mentally fit. It's fun to watch conures work out the "how" questions and the "which one" questions. Some birds seem to be engineers, seeking out problems such as untying knots and twisting wing nuts. Stores or catalogs may call things like these "puzzle" toys.

A small cardboard box of foot toys, playthings that your bird can pick up and manipulate with one foot, will keep his feet, beak, and tongue busy for hours. Similar mental stimulation comes from busy boards or abacus-style toys.

Action Toys
If you'd see it in an action flick—noise, destruction, and physical stunts of derring-do—that's how action toys engage birds. The noise of bells and parrot music boxes stimulates rock'em-sock'em, physical play that birds need.

Stainless steel food and water bowls are easy to clean and disinfect. A narday conure is pictured.

Everyday Life With Senior Birds

Dr. Greg Burkett, board-certified avian veterinarian, explains that human companions need to accommodate geriatric conures just as they would provide comfort and security for an aging grandparent.

"If a conure has stiff, arthritic, or deformed joints, these need to be considered when choosing the cage, perches, toys, playpens, food and water containers, and bedding." Make sure that all of these items are convenient for your mobility-impaired conure.

Feather loss in older birds affects their ability to regulate their temperatures. Accordingly, position your conure's cage so that the temperature is constant and comfortable for your elder bird. Your avian veterinarian may recommend a low-wattage heat lamp in some cases.

If your bird develops digestive problems or organ failure (liver or kidney failure is common in older birds), special diets are available.

The aging birds in Dr. Burkett's practice and the retired birds of the International Conure Association's (ICA) member breeders adjust well, even when eye diseases claim their sight. Important for the comfort of a conure losing his sight is consistent placement of food, water, and toys in his cage. If you keep objects in the location that your conure remembers, you and your avian companion can enjoy many more happy years together.

For sheer physicality, nothing beats your conure's flapping to power the whirling of an acrylic or rope mobile. Swings, ladders, and knotted ropes are also toys that stimulate his action.

Pyrrhura breeders comment that these "quiet conures" like to play on the bottom of their cages with balls and foot toys.

Comfort Toys

After a busy day, conures need some slowing down time. This is the time that your bird will chew woven palm strands or preen cotton rope and retreat to a sleep hut for privacy. You are also an excellent comfort toy. When your bird has calmed down after his physical play, have him sit on your knee or on a towel next to you. You can read or chat. Your conure may chatter back at you.

Toys to Destroy

Conures need to gnaw; it's in their nature. Try providing sticks of various sizes on which your bird can gnaw, which he will consider toys. Other toys to destroy are available for purchase. Or if you're ambitious, you can make toys to destroy yourself.

To keep conure beaks honed and psyches happy, provide a supply of these toys. As your friend destroys one set, supply the next. Think of these toys as essential to your conure's health as food. Don't look at the dwindling supply as a cost. Look at the reduction of the toy to toothpicks and dust as a game to play with your conure kid. Which toy will he go for first? Toothpicks or dust? Make this a family game. Safe conure chew toys that you have at home include old telephone books (remove the glossy cover first), adding machine paper, and cardboard boxes.

Untreated, unsprayed tree branches with bark and leaves attached are also excellent diversions. The American Society for the Prevention of Cruelty to Animals (ASPCA) has a website that provides a list of nontoxic plants that you can use as a guide for selecting safe chewing items. (See resources section) Some safe plants that you may have in your yard include roses, eucalyptus, and willow. Be sure that your plants have not been treated for pests with systemic poisons, because this will make them toxic.

If you're concerned about the cleanliness or suitability of a plant material, don't use it. To eliminate bacteria and some other pests from wood, treat branches in a solution of 1 part bleach to 25 parts water for 15 minutes and then rinse with plenty of fresh water and leave to dry. Another

Conures need plenty of toys to keep them contented—although probably not this many.

technique is to bake the branches in an oven at 200°F (93.3°C) for 20 minutes.

Manufactured Toys

Cholla, sisal, palm fronds, and softwood blocks are common materials for toys to destroy. You can buy toys assembled from these materials, or you can buy the materials and make them yourself.

Perches

Because birds stand day and night, foot condition is important to their comfort and health. Perches are a place of rest and comfort as well as a place for foot exercise. Wild birds stand on perches of every conceivable size, material, and texture, so providing variety of perch sizes is the first key to health. Varying perch diameters and materials exercises the feet, varies the pressure across the different parts of the foot, and keeps the skin of the feet and nails evenly worn. All perches can and should be washed carefully and disinfected each week.

Diameter

In an environment with a limited number of surfaces, the diameter of the perches needs to be appropriate to foot size. For the main perches, the rule of thumb is that the parrot's foot should encircle the perch with a gap of about 1/4 inch (0.6 cm) between the front and back nails of the foot. This gap allows the nails to rub the perch, keeping them short. If the perches are too small, the nails will grow too long.

Materials

Each perch material has its own advantages and disadvantages. Natural wood perches may be ideal for your conure because the size varies in a single perch. Multiple varying branch sizes accomplish two things: The bird chooses what size fits best, and his feet get the exercise they need to stay healthy. Keep in mind that wood perches need frequent replacement as your conure chews through them. Also, be sure to use untreated branches for your perches if you gather them yourself. Suppliers sell gizmos that securely affix natural branches to cage bars.

If you purchase perches, consider manzanita for one material. Although it can be slick, manzanita lasts longer than any other material except concrete. Concrete perches, available from your pet store or catalog, can be useful as an alternative perch placed lower in the cage. This will provide a place where your bird can hone his beak.

Flexible braided rope perches are nice for variety and for adding perches in a section of the cage that requires a nonlinear approach. Although these perches are difficult to clean, the work is worth it. Be sure to dry braided perches thoroughly after disinfecting. Snip off any frayed pieces to prevent your pet from becoming entangled in them.

Perches that are not appropriate include sandpaper or grooming

Conure-Strength Toys

A significant problem for many conure companions is choosing toys that are appropriate and safe for the strength of their bird. Lots of cute plastic toys were developed for parakeets, but toys appropriate for these animals may not be appropriate for conures. Your conure's beak and feet can crack a parakeet toy; sharp edges cause injury. Strong toys that challenge physical prowess and balance are needed to keep your conure in good physical condition.

Clean, nontoxic branches and leaves make fun toys for conures to shred.

the more often you will clean your cage. One trick with newspaper is to layer the sheets so that the top layer pulls off all in one go. This allows you to do a quick cleanup to remove the remains of food or heavy droppings to neaten the cage without a full cleaning.

Because your conure may chew the newspaper, use the newsprint sections rather than the slick advertisement sections. Newsprint ink is not harmful in the quantities to which your bird is exposed.

For bedding, avoid kitty litter, corncobs, crushed walnut shells, grit, sand, wood shavings, and artificial grass. These bedding materials provide poor dropping visuals and are possibly harmful if ingested.

perches. Sanitizing sandpaper perches is not possible. In addition, the surface can rub raw patches on your bird's foot, the first step toward serious foot problems.

Bedding

The simplest and best bedding is newspaper. Readily available, it absorbs enough of the droppings to be effective but leaves the impression of the droppings intact. This is important, because the quality of your bird's droppings is an effective monitor of his health.

When you choose your cage, try to select one that can accommodate a standard-sized newspaper. Folding and cutting newspaper to fit is a nuisance. The easier your bedding is to replace,

Grooming Supplies

If you are a first-time bird owner, grooming is a task that you should learn from professionals, including your veterinarian. When you have some experience watching and assisting in grooming, invest in some small, maneuverable scissors, a bird nail scissors, a grinding tool or hand file, and styptic powder. (See Chapter 4 for more information on grooming.)

Cuttlebone

Every cage used to come with a cuttlebone because birds were, once upon a time, fed an all-seed diet. Now that we have new, well-balanced diets, cuttlebone and mineral blocks should be used only upon the advice of your veterinarian.

Cage Cover

Most conures do best when their companions cover their cages at night, particularly in households where activity continues late. As mentioned earlier, your conure needs 12 hours of quiet private time every night for rest and sleep.

Covers range from custom-made with monograms to an old sheet drape. What's important is that the coverings are washable, provide adequate ventilation, and create a dark environment for your friend. Even with a sleeping hut—a cozy piece of cage furniture for your conure to roost in at night—he will appreciate the additional privacy that a cage cover provides. Sleeping huts do provide fun and security for the smaller conures. In fact, many play "peek-a-boo" with their companions, peering in and out of the sleeping hut. (Lots of conures are comics who make games of everything.)

Cage Cleaning

Daily cleaning is important, but good cage maintenance requires periodic deep cleaning and disinfection. Assembling a bucket of tools may make the chore easier. Basics include mild soap, a bristled brush for scrubbing small places, washcloths, and a disinfectant for use after cleaning.

Most people do not realize that disinfectants do not work until they remove the organic material (that is, bird droppings). Once you've cleaned and dried your bird's cage, use the disinfectant. You can buy commercial

Homemade Toys

If you're short of toys, it's easy to make some inexpensive ones. Thread folded newspaper into a "U" shape through the cage bars to create newspaper chews. Tuck subscription cards from magazines into an unused envelope to make a "mailbox" that your bird will investigate.

Clip garden vegetables or bird-safe plants (roses, butterfly bush, or grape vines) and hang them from the cage bars for shredding fun. Present your conure with a treasure box made from a paper bag or unwaxed paper cups with a nut inside.

Inexpensive interactive toys include a paper ball to toss back and forth or a knotted paper towel to use as a bird tickler.

disinfectants formulated for cage cleaning. An alternative is a bleach solution consisting of one part bleach to nine parts water. Wipe the bleach solution onto the cage, perches, and dishes. Let stand for 15 minutes. Rinse, wipe, and dry. Don't forget to clean and disinfect your bird's toys, too.

Your Conure's Daily Needs

Your conure needs what every living creature needs each day. First is an environment free from fear of predation and hunger. Next, your conure needs your company and attention—both concentrated attention and ambient attention. Third, your conure needs consideration for the time that he's going to be alone

during the day, including a rich group of toys and activities to stimulate him mentally and physically. Last, your conure needs limits, including an enforced bedtime.

Birds are creatures of habit. A schedule reassures your bird. He feels secure when he wakes, eats, bathes, roosts, and plays at the same times each day. Of course, variation is fine, but a core schedule makes life less stressful for you and your bird. You'll see fewer behavior problems as an added bonus.

Daily Bird Routine

Daily cycles of light and dark affect an animal's biology. Biological clocks, called circadian rhythms, match the daily 24-hour cycle of the earth's rotation on its axis. Birds have a rhythm of metabolism, body temperature, and alertness that follow the rhythm of the day. As a result, birds become active as the sun rises, at which point they gather food, drink, bathe themselves, and attend to flock business until midday, when they rest. Birds become active again at about 3:00 p.m., gathering food, drinking, and preening before the 12 hours of darkness, during which time they sleep.

Companion bird experts suggest supporting your bird's natural timetable as much as is practical for the happiness of both human and bird companions.

Natural branches make excellent conure perches. They help keep your conure's feet healthy.

FAMILY-FRIENDLY TIP

Involving Family Members in Conure Care

The more each member of the family is involved, the more devoted that family member will be in figuring out how to share the work. The abilities of the helper are important.

Task	Young Children	Older Children	Adults
Finding information about conures	Look at bird books and magazines. Pick out pictures that look like your bird.	Internet and library searches.	Join an exotic bird club.
Cage selection	Accompany parent to store to look at cages.	Measure cage size and bar spacing during shopping.	Identify local and online suppliers for cages.
Sleeping cages	Accompany parent in taking conure to sleeping cage. Sing a bedtime song for a conure.	Take conure to sleeping cage each night and complete the bedtime routine.	Supervise conure bedtime routine.
Play tops and gyms	Name the toys that your conure enjoyed the most that day. Pick up toys.	Help adult do a quick cleaning of play areas and toys.	Be responsible for clearing up areas used during the day.
Cage cleaning	Push vaccum to pick up debris around cage.	Help adults wipe cage bars and change paper.	Ensure that cage is cleaned daily. Check that toy hangers are closed and doors are correctly latched.
Food and water bowls	Carry food and water bowls to cage.	Measure food into clean bowls.	Follow feeding schedule and change of water.
Bathing	Watch your conure bathe.	Use washcloth after bathing to wipe wet areas.	Make sure baths are offered at least twice weekly.
Toys	Choose between two toys of each type.	Arrange toys in cage, making sure one of each type is available.	Monitor safety of toy arrangement.
Disinfection	None. Sing with conure while older family members take care of this.	Help to assemble toys and perches after cleaning.	Wash and disinfect, explaining role of hand washing and disinfecting.

Chapter 3

Eating Well

Your conure's well-being, happiness, and long life depend on good nutrition. The quality of his feathers, temperament, and zest for life all come from being properly nourished. Veterinarians say that poor nutrition causes most companion bird health problems.

For companion birds, food, in addition to nutrition, provides choice and variety in your pet's daily life. It is vital to make sure that your conure's nutritional needs are met, as well as his food-related behavior needs.

Many keepers and veterinarians suggest a two-pronged dietary strategy relying on pelleted diets for at least 60 percent of a bird's nutrition and fresh foods for the remaining portion. If this sounds at odds with everything your mother taught you about feeding birds, that's natural. In the past, bird owners purchased a bag of seed, a cuttlebone, and a mineral block. Today's researchers investigate the specific needs of different companion bird species, rather than limiting avian nutrition research to chickens and ducks. As a result of this new research, we know that seed-based diets limit companion birds to one-fifth of their natural lifespan. Many birds, of course, prefer eating seed over all other foods. As with people, though, a diet of preferred foods is not the basis for a healthy body.

Components of Good Nutrition

Conures require a mixture of proteins, carbohydrates, fats, vitamins, and minerals. Presenting those essential nutrients in a way your bird enjoys ensures that you've done your best for his health. In other words, provide healthy food that your bird is eager to eat. Most experts agree that the essential nutrition for a companion bird comes from clean, fresh water; and the daily addition of fresh fruits, vegetables, protein, and small amounts of seed.

The Role of Water

A bird's body is approximately 80 percent water, and it provides the lubrication for his entire system. Without it, he can't produce energy,

Exercise

Part of a healthy lifestyle is exercise. Each bird is different, and some birds may require encouragement to exercise.

Exercise for birds means out-of-the-cage wing flapping, toy punching, and heart-rate raising. You and your conure can develop games to be a part of this exercise. Some conure's catch paper balls and fling them back at you. Others attack a dangling toy, flap their wings, and ride the toy like a kid on a merry-go-round.

move nutrients around his body, or regulate his temperature.

Although you may not see your bird drinking, he does so several times each day. Most birds drink in the morning and again at night before sleep. Clean, fresh drinking water should be available to your bird at all times.

Pelleted Diets

High-quality pellets ensure a proper nutrition base, eliminating much of the uncertainty that pet companions have in ensuring a proper diet. The best suppliers blend diets based on research into species-specific nutrition. As dog and cat dietary needs differ, so do conure diets differ from those for cockatoos or parakeets.

Pelleted diets are manufactured in a wide range of qualities, from the bulk bin at your pet store to premium diets available only from your veterinarian or specialty store. The advantage of these pelleted diets as a base for your conure is the knowledge that he has all the nutrients he needs. The pellet form also answers the problem of your bird picking through the food, selecting only those bits he wants. With pellets, you know that your bird is eating the nutrients he needs.

Supplementation, if you're using a correctly formulated diet, is usually unnecessary. In fact, adding vitamins and minerals could harm

How Wild Conures Eat

In foraging groups, wild birds select among seasonal flowers and tree buds, insects, fruits, and seeds. After they eat what's ripe, they move on to the next tree where the produce is fresh.

Conures forage in flocks, and they teach their young birds what is good to eat at different times of the year. As a human conure companion, you can use this inborn search for guidance to your advantage. When your bird is reluctant to try something that you feel he would enjoy, eat some in front of your conure, and make a fuss about how delicious the morsel is.

Forshaw's *Parrots of the World* and Arndt's *Atlas of Conures* provide excellent information on wild diets. You'll be amazed at the variety and kinds of foods that your conure eats in the wild.

You will not be able to duplicate your parrot's natural wild diet, because it would be impossible to obtain the plants and to grow them successfully. Even more important, the wild flocks may be eating whole categories of food that researchers are unaware of. Still, what comes through in reading these accounts is how varied the conures' diets are and how much time and care they devote to acquiring and eating healthy wild foods.

balance among these classes of nutrients gives your bird the proper nutrition.

Protein, essential for growth and disease resistance, builds the body's tissues. Your conure builds muscle from amino acids, the protein building blocks present in his diet. Beans and nuts are the usual sources of protein in formulated diets.

Carbohydrates are the fuel that gives the body energy. Carbohydrates, including starches and sugars, come from foods such as fruits, vegetables, and grains. Prepared diets usually contain plenty of vegetables and grains.

Fats store energy for the body. In addition, fats are necessary in the body's use of vitamins A, D, E, and K. Nuts and seeds are common sources of fats.

Vitamins regulate many body processes. Your conure needs 13 essential vitamins that are included in a good diet. Different vitamins are found in various foods, with fresh vegetables being a particularly good source for a wide range of them.

Minerals have jobs to do in maintaining bone integrity and normal function of nerves, muscles, and body fluid balance. A properly formulated diet includes all the minerals your conure needs.

your bird. Add supplements like cuttlebone, mineral blocks, and whole minerals only upon the advice of your veterinarian. To provide the best nutrition, buy the best quality diet available, one that's packaged and distributed with freshness as a priority.

Pelleted Foods—Pros and Cons

Good pelleted food is expensive, but you'll feed the pellets in small amounts because the nutrition is very dense. Many veterinarians recommend that pellets make up 60 percent of your bird's diet, although a few suggest pellets as a smaller part of a diet rich in fresh foods.

Composition

Formulated pellets include a mix of proteins, carbohydrates, and fats. The

Healthy Foods for Conures

Greens: chard, mustard, sorrel, cilantro, parsley, kale, collards, carrot tops, rapini, endive, arugula

Vegetables: celery, bell pepper, squash, cauliflower, cabbage, carrot, beet, yam, pumpkin, snow pea, broccoli, kohlrabi, potato, cooked beans (e.g., garbanzo, kidney, peas, limas, black-eyed peas)

Fruits: apple, lemon, orange, grape, berries, banana, pear, plum, mango, cantaloupe, melons, papaya, fig

Pasta: various shapes, whole grain (wheat, spelt, etc.)

Grains: brown rice, barley, millet, amaranth, quinoa, farina, oats, corn

Nuts: brazil nut, almond, walnut, pine nut, filbert, cashew, nut butters

Protein: tofu, chicken, salmon

Dairy: yogurt, cheese (small amounts)

Qualities of Pelleted Diets

Selecting correctly sized pellets for your bird's beak is important. Macaws, for example, eat much larger pellets than conures. Generally, good-quality pellets are marked for the appropriate species.

In addition, the form of pelleted diets varies. Companions can choose among pellets, crumbles, balls, and square-shaped cakes. Some people blend different formulations to give variety to their conure's pellet cup.

Manufacturers often offer colored pellets to make nuggets more appealing to birds and human shoppers. However, coloring the food is not necessary. Further, the long-term effects of food dyes are of concern to many veterinarians. Pellets colored with natural dyes, such as beet juice, are preferable.

Selecting a Manufactured Diet

Once you have decided to feed a manufactured diet for your conure, the work of selecting one begins. A good source of information is your breeder, and the International Conure Association (ICA) has members experienced in the feeding and rearing of healthy birds similar to yours.

Several avian diets are available only from veterinarians or from the manufacturer directly, to ensure freshness. Consider these top-quality suppliers. If you are considering a diet other than that offered by your veterinarian, examine the labels carefully. Discuss the choice, based on the contents, with your veterinarian.

Fresh Food

Fresh fruits, vegetables, protein, and small amounts of seed provide a satisfying visual experience, as well as natural foraging fun and the mental exercise of choosing which items to eat. Maneuvering, crunching, picking, and discarding textures and tastes that don't suit your conure give him a sensual experience and brain exercise.

You can present fresh foods in a variety of attractive ways. Some keepers hang greens around the cage so that their birds can strip the stalks like forest foliage. Other keepers use skewers to stack foods such as yam, banana, and mango. Your conure may eat the stack, use the skewered stack as a toy, or both.

Home-Cooked Diets

For variety, many bird keepers make home-cooked diets that include fresh-cooked beans, rice, corn, and pasta served with vegetables and poultry. (Some birds readily eat poultry as a source of protein. In the wild, insects provide protein to some conure species.) When feeding cooked food, remember that bacteria can grow in short periods. To ensure that your bird is safe, especially in hot weather, remove cooked foods after 30 to 45 minutes.

Why Feed Fruits and Vegetables?

Parrots benefit from vegetables, fruits, whole grains, and protein. Fresh organic foods, when you can get them, are best. Variety is key for conures. Unlike domestic household pets, conures—closer to their wild origins—instinctively spend a good deal of time foraging for food. Selecting ripe foods and eating take most of their early morning and late afternoon time. Greens, vegetables, fruits, pasta, grain, nuts, poultry and a small amount of yogurt or cheese can benefit your bird both mentally and physically.

What works best is to vary the presentation. One week you could chop chard into small pieces. The next week, offer chard whole from a skewer or threaded between the cage bars. Birds like variety, not only in what foods they eat but also in their presentation. Changing the form of the food, chopped to skewered, skewered to chopped, rolled in pellets, and cut in different shapes, entices your bird to expand his appreciation of different foods.

What Other Human Foods Are Good Choices?

Your conure wants to eat what you eat. Share a salad for dinner. If you eat

Be sure to buy pellets that are the right size for your conure.

broccoli, he will eat broccoli. If you eat a garbanzo bean, he will imitate you. Most human foods prepared from fresh ingredients and low in salt can be fed. Your nutritious family meal leftovers also can be suitable for your conure. If you feed dairy products, do not feed more than 1/2 teaspoon (2.5 ml) in one meal.

If you're ever in doubt about whether a certain item is bad for your conure, the American Society for the Prevention of Cruelty of Animals (ASPCA) maintains a list of foods that are poisonous for pets. Check the list at www.aspca.org as an authoritative but not complete source.

Selecting Your Conure's Fresh Foods

Fruits and Vegetables

Fruits and vegetables, for conures as for people, should be as clean and colorful as possible. Rather than regarding your bird as a consumer of your rejected produce, remember that your bird eats very little. It is not expensive to feed him well. Birds react to the soggy, the overripe, and the overcooked in the same way you do; the taste and texture isn't right, and they just don't like it. Unless you are using organic produce, scrub fruits and vegetables to remove pesticides or appearance-enhancing waxes. (This is a good practice for your own fruits and vegetables, too.)

Proportions for Fresh-Food Meals

Each meal of fresh food should be made up of a variety of tasty tidbits. Here's a rough guide to the proportions of the different types of fresh foods in a meal:
Fruit: 20 to 40%
Poultry and dairy: up to 5%
Seed: never more than 25%
Vegetables: 30 to 50%

Seeds

Other than purchasing them from a quality supplier, the best way to test seed freshness is to sprout them. Soaked in water for one or two days, seeds should begin to sprout. Seeds that take longer are not as fresh.

Most seed, even when it is carefully grown and processed, contains insect eggs. To ensure that insects do not hatch and consume your seeds, freeze them for at least 24 hours following purchase. To keep seed fresh, you may freeze it for up to six months, withdrawing small amounts as you need more for your conure.

Amount of Food

Keep in mind that the amount of food your bird eats each day doesn't vary much. Whether he eats properly or whether you provide a breakfast of seed full of calories and fat (the equivalent of doughnuts for birds), birds consume a set number of calories

and not more. If your bird focuses on the high-fat items first, he may absorb all the calories needed with these low-value foods and leave the good, nutritious foods in his dish.

Unlike wild birds who fly 100 or more miles (160.9 km) each day to forage, most companion birds get relatively little daily exercise; accordingly, their caloric requirements are lower.

Timing of Feeding

Conures need food available first thing in the morning and then again in the mid- to late afternoon as they prepare to roost for the night. Clean water must be available at all times.

Most keepers suggest feeding the nutritionally dense pelleted diets early in the day when a bird is most likely to be hungry. After a night of fasting, pellets in the morning will likely be eaten completely if you do not overfeed. Once the pellets are

consumed, offer fresh foods as entertainment and as a supplement. With 60 to 70 percent of the day's nutrition coming from a pellet diet, your conure has 30 to 40 percent of a balanced and varied diet to look forward to the rest of the day.

Translating Information Into Action

Putting information about conure diet into practice seems as though it might take forever. On the contrary. With a little practice and a routine, you will feed your conure in fine style in ten minutes a day. The keys are establishing a routine and having enough food and water dishes so that one set is always clean.

Daily Feeding Routine

Feed your conure twice each day and provide clean, fresh water morning and night. In the morning, feed the pellets and hang greens and other low-sugar foods for your bird to snack on during the day. In the evening, provide a mix of vegetables and fruits.

The problem most people have in feeding fresh fruits and vegetables is the preparation time required. Compounding this problem is the fact that conure feeding time is the late afternoon, when stressed families are coming home, making dinner, and otherwise bustling about. To solve this conflict, many keepers prepare a "conure salad" that will last for three to four days if refrigerated.

Conure Salad

Depending on the size of your conure, 2 to 3 cups (0.5 to 0.7 l) of conure salad every four days should provide enough fresh afternoon nutrition for all but the most voracious eater. What should be in the salad? Try thinking of the foods in five groups. Add equal amounts of the five parts. First, chop some greens—chard, mustard greens, kale, carrot tops, endive, collards, parsley, or other fresh herbs and leafy greens. Next, consider vegetables. Try celery, zucchini, bell peppers, sprouts, cabbage, beets, green beans, broccoli, and cauliflower. Use a layer of squash, yams, and carrots—the orange vegetables—and sprinkle a small amount of uncooked whole grain pasta on top. Cooked beans, especially the bean mixes, add nutrition, and your conure will love them. Cook these and store them separately until you are ready to serve. This keeps your greens and vegetables fresh longer.

For sweetness, add fresh sliced corn on the cob, chopped apple, unpeeled chopped citrus fruits, grapes, mango, and other fruits. Your conure will appreciate melon when available, and fresh seasonal berries are a treat. Storing the fruit separately keeps the moisture content of the greens lower, preventing spoilage.

Remove the mixture from your conure's cage before bedtime, and check the water again. A conure could survive for a day without food, but a constant supply of clean water is necessary each day.

Other Diet Information

Most of us feel compelled to feed our pets food that we eat because they beg. Conures beg as effectively as any dog can. What's important to remember is that conures beg because you are eating the food, and they are flock animals.

Foods to Avoid

Food that's fine for you in moderation can be deadly for your bird. Alcohol or caffeine in any form, as well as

Foods Harmful to Your Conure

Here is a list of foods and ingredients that should never be fed to your conure.
- alcohol
- avocado
- caffeine
- chocolate
- cured meats
- fatty or oily foods
- salty food (including salted nuts)
- sugared products

Conures enjoy millet, but it lacks many nutrients. Use it as a treat, not as a main part of your conure's diet.

chocolate, are toxic to your bird. Even small amounts are not acceptable. Cured meats, fatty and salted foods, like potato chips, and snack foods are off limits, no matter how much your bird begs. Similarly, sugared foods, including cookies, cakes, ice cream, and some cereals, are on the do-not-feed list.

No Need for Supplements

Vitamin or mineral supplements intended for sprinkling on food or adding to water are not necessary if you use a high-quality pelleted food. In fact, excessive vitamins and minerals can cause health problems. Use supplements only upon your veterinarian's advice.

The All-Seed Diet: an Unhealthy Choice

Birds love seed, and many would eat it to the exclusion of all other food items. However, seeds lack important nutrients and contain as much as 50 percent fat. Aside from the excessive amounts of fat that seeds contain, they lack nutrients necessary for a healthy life: two critical amino acids, ten important vitamins, and many minerals and trace minerals. Fed exclusively on seeds, a bird's health suffers and he becomes unwilling to eat anything else. Feed only a small amount of seed as part of a healthy varied diet.

Grit

Many people believe that feeding grit to birds is crucial for digestion. This idea comes from raising poultry. Chickens eat whole seeds, requiring small bits of grit to grind off the coating. Conures, who remove the hulls and eat only the soft inner matter, do not crush seeds in their digestive tracts, so they do not benefit from grit in their diet. Many avian veterinarians in the United States advise against feeding grit, believing it is at best unhelpful and at worst harmful for conures and other parrots.

Changing Diets

If your conure has been raised on a limited, unhealthy diet, the time that you spend converting him to an improved diet will be worthwhile. Older birds can be especially resistant because their tastes have developed over many years.

During the conversion process, it's important to monitor your bird's weight. (A postal scale or food scale will do the job.) A 10-percent weight loss for a bird is cause to contact your veterinarian.

The most difficult problem in changing diets is teaching your conure that the items you present are food. Birds often do not identify the pellets or the greens that you offer as food. Birds learn what to eat from other flock members, so one excellent way to encourage your picky eater to try new things is to dine with him.

Another method of conversion is to use the diet that your bird is used to, but incorporate the new diet into the bowl. Although your bird may pick and choose the bits he is used to, he will become accustomed to seeing the new foods.

Coating the new foods with strained carrots or applesauce is another approach. Teach your bird to put the food into his mouth with an irresistible coating. Stirring pellets in a favored soft food is a great way to entice him to sample the new pellets, learn that they are food, and make the desired switch. Although this method is not a good long-term solution, pureed fruits and vegetables or fruit juice-soaked pellets trigger learning and will eventually work with even the most stubborn eater.

Be consistent and patient. You'll waste some pellets, but one day you'll notice your bird trying new foods without your special efforts.

Feed your conure twice a day, in the morning and in the late afternoon or early evening.

Chapter 4

Looking Good

Grooming conures refers to the care of the feathers, nails, and beak and is not just about appearance. It makes a difference in the health, well-being, and companionability of your bird. Grooming is about the health of the most defining aspects of the bird: his feathers, beak, and nails. Although your bird grooms all his feathers, his nails, and his beak every day, you should give a big assist twice each year with flight feathers and nails.

About Feathers

Birds' bodies have several types of feathers, each with a different job. As your bird "drops" feathers, save one of each type so that you (and your kids, if you have any) can compare how each type looks and feels.

Long feathers attached to the wing, called primary feathers, provide the lift for flight. A completely different structure, a small, delicate contour feather, covers the bird's torso. Snowflake-shaped down feathers, the layer under contour feathers, insulate the bird. Unlike the random hair growth across mammals' skin, feathers grow in straight lines, or tracts, across a bird's body.

Contour or Body-Covering Feathers

The type of feathers that cover a bird's body are called contour feathers. Contour feathers grow in distinct tracts, or lines, fanning out to cover his bare areas. A complicated network of muscle fibers connects the bases of the contour feathers, allowing the bird a sophisticated degree of feather movement.

Birds can fluff up body feathers to increase insulation and sleek them down for cooling. Birds also raise and lower patches of feathers as part of a display or behavioral signal.

Daily Feather Care

A healthy bird grooms each feather each day. Your conure preens at a quiet time, such as mid-day. Working one feather at a time, he slides his beak along the feather shaft, removing debris and "rehooking" the tiny feather barbules, like zipping a zipper, so that the feather regains its sturdy surface.

A gland at the base of your bird's tail produces the oil that he uses to condition and waterproof his feathers. Normally, your bird rubs his beak along the gland to gather oil before attending to a new group of feathers. During preening, the beak spreads oil as he preens his feathers. Whether or not your bird bathes every day, he devotes hours to grooming.

Preening New Feathers

At least once each year and usually twice, your bird loses and replaces feathers until every feather on his body is new. New feathers erupt through the skin wrapped in a cuticle-like sheath. A conure living as a companion needs help in grooming the feather sheaths on his head and neck, spots that even his flexible neck do not allow him to reach. This process can be a source of bonding between you and your bird.

Be careful to wait until the feather has matured completely. "Blood feathers," as they are called, are fragile; your touching them hurts him. When the feather matures, usually within a week, your bird will be anxious for your preening help. Mature feathers will be the same length as the feathers on either side of them. The base of the feather shaft will look thin and empty, rather than the plump, dark appearance it had when it was just beginning to grow.

Petting in Reverse

Rather than smoothing your conure's feathers in the direction they grow (the way you stroke a dog or cat's head), most birds prefer having their neck and head feathers delicately rubbed in the opposite direction. Try gently moving your fingernail across your bird's cheek, rubbing "against the grain." The movement is similar to plucking a string in slow motion.

A Feather Don't

Never put shampoo or lotion or dust any foreign substance on your bird's feathers. Feather appearance, a reflection of your bird's physical and psychological health, comes from his diet and natural inclination to groom. If his

feathers look unhealthy or dirty, visit your veterinarian. Carelessness about appearance is a sure sign of illness, not a sign that your bird needs shampoo.

Flight Feather Clipping

One of the most controversial subjects among bird companions and trainers is the trimming of flight feathers—sometimes incorrectly called "wing trims" (the wing is not surgically altered)—to prevent flight. Untrimmed flight feathers, experts say, are the

The Expert Knows

What Is Molting?

Molting is the process of losing old feathers and replacing them with new ones. Day length, temperature, and food supply affect the hormones that control molting. Before a new feather can grow, the old one must fall out. New feathers begin as a thickened projection of skin. The pin or blood feathers appear within days, wrapped in a protective sheath. When growth is completed, the artery and vein supplying the nutrients close. The bird preens away the protective sheath.

Birds do not molt all at once. Over about six weeks, feathers drop in an orderly pattern. Birds in the wild usually molt twice each year. During the molt, birds need extra protein and are not as resistant to disease.

primary reason for escape and accidental death in companion birds. Trimming undoubtedly keeps companion birds safer, but it does deprive them of normal flight and requires the companion to ensure her conure get adequate exercise.

Pros and Cons

The trouble with flight feather clipping is that new parrot companions are often unsure that they should clip until it's too late, and their conure escapes or is injured. The goal of a proper clip is to limit flight to slow, descending glides.

This shortening of the wing feathers allows a decent chance of retrieving a bird who finds his way outside. Startled birds with flight feathers trimmed are unlikely to gain enough speed to injure themselves if they bolt and hit a glass window or door. Still another reason is to maintain order. If you are a novice bird handler, you need to be able to pick up your bird with a reasonable expectation that he will stay on your hand. This is especially important when training or when having behavior conflicts. A conure who is the most delightful companion when

his flight feathers are clipped can transform into an airborne knife-beaked devil when fully flighted.

Some companions don't believe in wing trims because they wish their birds to be in as natural a state as possible. Others believe that their bird is so tame that escape is all but impossible. Others feel that the trim affects the relationship between companion and bird in a negative way.

If you choose to leave your bird's flight feathers unclipped, make sure that you have double doors to prevent accidental escape; also, put markers of some sort on all window glass so that your bird perceives a solid wall instead of open skies. Finally, be sure to microchip your bird (always a good idea) so that there is some chance of his return.

Conures, such as this white-eyed, enjoy being pet on the neck against the direction of the feathers.

Grooming Frequency

Grooming is a process, not something that you do once and can forget. Here's a chart showing how often you will need to perform grooming chores.

Process	Frequency	Who Does This Grooming?
Bathing	Every day or two is ideal	Any family member
Preening	Every two or three days	Any family member
Nail trims and feather clips	Usually twice each year, but depends on individual bird	Veterinarian or veterinary technician recommended

Wing Feather Trims

Trimming your companion bird's flight feathers is something that you do at least twice each year because the feathers drop out and are replaced by new ones. Wild birds' flight feathers are worn by flying. You can see the wear on the edge of the feathers where repeated rubbing against the air dulls them. Because mating requires brilliant, well-conditioned feathers, most birds molt twice each year. Molting replaces flight feathers, usually in the same feather positions on the left and right wings at one time.

You will know that your bird is molting when you see long, strong feathers at the bottom of his cage. You also may notice new flight feathers appearing on your bird. At first covered by a waxy-looking sheath, the feather develops and unfolds when your bird preens away this sheath. Once all your conure's new flight feathers have come in, it's time for a wing trim, a part of the grooming process.

Trimming flight feathers is an art. The goal is to trim just enough primary feathers to keep the bird from rising in flight. However, he should be able to make a controlled glide from a high place to the floor.

Your groomer or veterinarian should inspect the wing for blood feathers. Blood feathers are those still growing, and they are called blood feathers because they receive blood from the feather follicle until the feather is mature. When it matures, this natural process stops the blood supply. Once the blood supply stops, the feather can be safely trimmed.

Grooming Nails

Nails should remain sharp enough that your conure can grip perches well but not sharp enough to hurt or poke holes in your skin. Like dogs, birds have a blood supply to the nail. Many vets

Looking Good

Trim just enough feathers to prevent your conure from flying up and away.

use emery boards to restore a proper shape after clipping the nail. Some experienced groomers use a grinding tool either as a substitute for clipping or to reshape the nail after clipping. You should attempt nail clipping only after an experienced person—vet, groomer, or fellow bird companion—shows you how.

Finding an Experienced Groomer

Finding someone who knows how to trim your bird's feathers and nails properly is essential. Clipping flight feathers requires consideration of the bird's individual habits, his body type, and his physical condition.

One excellent resource for bird grooming is your veterinarian. She and her technician can trim flight feathers appropriately, avoiding the significant injuries that follow incorrect wing trims. Her veterinary technician will restrain your bird in a gentle, safe manner while the vet works on the actual trimming. Most avian or exotic animal vets are happy to trim wing feathers and toenails.

An advantage of having the veterinarian groom your bird is the opportunity that she has to observe his general health. If she sees a reason for concern, the problem can be discussed and addressed on the same visit. Most veterinarians' rates for grooming are comparable to professional groomers. Also, you'll have a qualified professional evaluate how many flight feathers to trim.

Professional Groomers

Many people advertise professional bird grooming services, but there are no accreditations or professional guidelines in this field. You, then, must determine whether the groomer has the experience to do a good job. This is another reason to start with your veterinarian and have her teach you the principles of good wing trims.

If you feel uncomfortable about

what is happening to your bird during grooming, speak up. Grooming may annoy your bird, but it should not terrify him. The stress of a poor grooming experience can kill birds.

Discuss with the groomer the procedure for capture and restraint of your bird in advance. Also, discuss the tools and the extent of the grooming, keeping in mind that individual birds require different treatment.

Bathing Benefits

Much of a bird's life is about keeping his feathers clean. Your conure must clean, lubricate, and properly place 2,000 to 3,000 feathers in their correct positions each day. Providing bathing opportunities assists him in his preening. Especially with the drying effects of heating systems, companion birds' skin can become dry and itchy.

The How of Bird Bathing

Think about wild birds bathing. A bird dips his beak and then his head into a shallow pool of water. Raising his head, wings fluttering, the bird directs water back over his body. Other birds stand in a soaking mist, droplets dripping from the leaves. These are natural bathing methods. Take advantage of your conure's natural tendencies.

Individual birds have a "bathing preference." Some conures like to be "spritzed" with a gentle mist of water from a spray bottle. Aim your sprayer above him, letting the mist settle on his feathers as a damp fog might. Other conures jump into any vessel filled with water—including the shallow crockery bowl or plate filled with lukewarm water intended for his bath.

Whatever the bathing method, supervision is necessary. In addition, your companion should be completely dry before perching for the night.

Techniques and Equipment

There are several different methods for bathing conures. Try each one and see which one yours likes best. Go slowly, and make sure that your bird does not become frightened.

You can use a towel to help restrain your conure during nail trimming.

FAMILY-FRIENDLY TIP
Kids and Grooming

Kids can take an active role in keeping your conure looking good. Bathing is an excellent way to involve kids of elementary school age and older in conure grooming. Once you know that your bird is not afraid of these bathing methods, ask your kids to try them.

Spritz overhead: Using a spray bottle, kids can create a gentle mist that falls onto your conure's head. Kids have fun asking the conure how he likes the rain.

The sink bath: Some conures love to get in a puddle of water and take a bath. If yours does, have your kids take him to a clean sink and run 1 inch (2.5 cm) of room temperature water. Ask them to report to you what happens. All of you may be surprised. (Be sure that your kids know that no soap is allowed!)

The foliage bath: Have your kids take leaves that you recommend, such as spinach, chard, lettuce, or maybe even carrot tops. Have them wash the leaves and present them to your conure. Many conures love to rub on wet leaves.

The steam bath: Most birds love to perch just outside the shower spray, letting the damp air moisten their skin and feathers. Kids can take turns showering with their conure. For the kid who hates to shower, this could be just the trick to get her to like it.

Cage Bottom

Use a shallow earthenware bowl or plate with lukewarm water in the bottom of the cage. Earthenware makes the bowl too heavy for your bird to overturn. Some conure keepers suggest bathing your bird in the morning before you replace the paper.

Dip your fingers into the water and exclaim with delight. Your bird will likely follow. Remember, birds are flock creatures. They may not step into the bath, but most perch on the edge, submerge their heads, toss water over their backs, and fluff their feathers.

Greens

Some birds like bathing in wet branches or leaves. Place fresh greens on a plate at the bottom of the cage. Spray the leaves. Your bird may come down and rub his feathers against the leaves.

Spray Bottle

Some birds prefer warm, gentle spray from a water bottle. Spray the air above your bird. Think perfume atomizer instead of power washer for the spray setting. Spray the water on yourself to demonstrate and habituate your bird to the sound.

Showering With Your Bird

Some birds enjoy showering with their favorite person. The first time, clear the bathroom counter and allow your bird to perch there to observe. His reaction tells you how long the familiarization process may take. (Familiarization takes about two weeks for most birds.) Some birds are anxious to join you on the first day. Meanwhile, the warm, moist shower air is good for your bird's skin. If he likes the shower, try a perch that affixes securely to a shower fixture. Be sure to keep all soaps and shampoos out of reach.

Cautions

Things to avoid include battering your bird with the full spray from showers. In addition, some birds have been disciplined with spray from a water bottle (not recommended!). These birds should not be sprayed for bathing purposes. Also, no bird should be allowed in water deeper than his feet unsupervised.

Your approach to bathing has a great effect on how your

bird will react. Integrate the water into something fun, a morning ritual that you have with your bird. Talk enthusiastically about the experience. "Isn't this fun? I love baths. Want to shower?" If you have fun, chances are your bird will, too.

Sunlight

Light plays important roles in the daily and annual cycles of a bird. Sunlight regulates the metabolic and seasonal clock, provides a sense of well-being, and supports birds' physical development.

Daily Light Requirements

Light regulates the rhythm of a conure's day. Most wild conures live near the earth's equator, where daylight and night are roughly equal in length. In the wild, they leave the roost in the morning to forage. They

Give your conure the opportunity to bathe three times weekly.

Looking Good

sleep or preen quietly at midday and then have several hours of active foraging and socializing before roosting again at dusk. In guiding this cycle, sunlight bolsters your conure's mental and physical condition.

Sunlight stimulates preening, the process of conditioning each feather each day. Sunlight also helps to break down old feather oils and to spread new oil, reduce bacteria, and expose parasites for removal.

Conures also use ultraviolet (UV) light to assist in synthesizing vitamin D, which their bodies cannot absorb but must manufacture.

Seasonal Behaviors

Besides the rhythm of daily behavior, light provides cues for your conure's seasonal behavior. Hormones induced by the seasonal variations in daylight hours stimulate molting and breeding.

Birds who produce feathers during the molt replace up to 10 percent of their body mass. This process of feather development benefits from the nutritional and metabolic effects of adequate sunlight.

Light-Producing Equipment

A balanced avian visual spectrum includes ultraviolet light. Windows filter out the ultraviolet light and allow visible light to pass through. This means that placing your bird in a sunny window will not provide the entire spectrum that he needs. Be sure that

My Bird Won't Bathe

Some birds have not experienced bathing and may not be inclined to try. Entice your companion by using his desire to be a member of the flock. Using a shallow plate, dangle your fingers in the water. Make a game of tossing small treats into the water so that your bird steps onto the plate. Make it fun and exciting. Expect that you may not succeed for a week to ten days.

your bird can escape full sun and the resulting heat. Conures can become severely overheated from sun through a window, even on a moderate temperature day.

To provide the light that your bird needs indoors, use full-spectrum fluorescent lights. Incandescent lights (lightbulbs with filaments that glow) do not meet the standard needed for birds. Several manufacturers make lights that meet the standard. On the packaging, look for fine print mentioning "full spectrum with a color rendition index (CRI) > 90 and color temperature (CT) > 5000." Your local or online bird supplier can advise you on availability and pricing. Some lights that meet these standards are manufactured to provide ultraviolet light for reptiles.

Position full-spectrum lights overhead for greatest effect, remembering that your bird sees into the blue and violet range (which you don't), so the environment looks brighter to your bird than to you. For maximum effect, position the lights so that your bird's usual perch is 12 to 18 inches (30.5 to 45.7 cm) from the light.

These special lights also have electronic ballasts to eliminate flicker that birds notice but you don't. To duplicate consistent photoperiod rhythms, use timers. Ideally, have your timer turn on lights one hour after sunrise and off an hour before dusk. Adjust timers every two to four weeks to the shortening or lengthening days. At minimum, recommended light use is an hour each day.

How to Use the Out-of-Doors

When temperatures permit, taking companion birds outside can help their physiology and psychology. In taking your companion out-of-doors, the first rule is safety. Pet birds outdoors must be (1)

caged or leashed, (2) have a wing clip, and (3) be supervised. If you can't do all three, don't take your bird outside. Conures are excellent flyers and can sometimes fly even with proper primary feather trims.

One quiet afternoon when you and your bird are alone, take the cage that he lives in outside. If it is too large, use your smaller travel cage. Plan in advance where you'll position your bird. Before moving the cage containing him outside, cover the entire thing with a towel. Place the enclosure on a table or other sturdy surface, or hang it from a sturdy tree branch to prevent curious predators' investigation. Keep in mind that cats, dogs, or snakes can overturn or stalk the cage, frightening or injuring your bird. This is a huge reason why you must supervise your bird out-of-doors.

Once the cage is outside and positioned, fold the drape back to cover only a portion of the cage top. This helps your bird to feel secure. Birds assume that trouble can come from any direction, and they hide from trouble as a defense. Denied this opportunity, your conure may become frantic.

Remember that the sun moves and temperatures change over a few minutes. Your conure will be okay with temperatures no lower than 55°F (12.8°C) and no higher than 85°F (29.4°C).

Seasonal variations in light cause physical and behavioral changes in conures, such as molting.

Chapter 5

Feeling Good

Properly nourished and exercised conures are likely to grow up healthy. Even so, an annual well-bird examination is a good investment in your conure's care. You'll probably never have an emergency, but in case one does occur, having a plan is a good thing. Having the equipment, the knowledge, and the procedure in place makes coping with the unexpected easier. The linchpin in your conure's well care and in his emergency care is your veterinarian.

Your Avian Veterinarian

Although you set the tone for your companion's care, your veterinarian is an essential advisor, not only for treating illness but also for diet, nutrition, and exercise advice. She can also be a conduit to the other service providers you need.

Choosing a veterinarian takes thought and time. Because most pets are dogs and cats, most veterinarians are accustomed to these animals, but most are not experienced in treating birds. Those who do are called avian veterinarians or exotic animal veterinarians. Veterinarians specializing in birds usually are not more expensive than vets who specialize in dogs and cats. There are simply fewer of them.

Signs That Your Conure Is Sick

If your conure shows any of these signs, you should seek veterinary advice.
- change in behavior
- change in droppings
- drooping wings
- eyes mostly or completely closed
- fluffed up feathers
- loss of appetite
- regurgitation

A good place to start your search is the Association of Avian Veterinarians (www.aav.org). Many excellent veterinarians who treat birds are not certified avian veterinarians; in fact, only a small number have taken the extensive series of tests required for this certification. Your state association of veterinary medicine will have a list of practices that regularly see birds. Local exotic bird clubs usually keep a list of veterinarians with extensive avian experience, too, and club members will have information about the various practice personalities.

After-Hours Emergency Clinics

A second resource that you need is an after-hours emergency clinic. Once the emergency occurs, you won't have

Providing veterinary care when needed is part of being a conscientious conure companion.

time to shop around for a clinic. Sick and injured birds are fragile and require immediate attention.

Your veterinarian should recommend a competent source of after-hours treatment for birds in her care. Interview the after-hours clinics that she recommends. Emphasize your need for bird care, and question the staff closely about the vets' experience with birds. If you are very lucky, your avian veterinarian will offer this service herself.

Your Conure's Annual Examination

Your bird's first annual examination is the one that you'll do at the time of purchase. Each year thereafter, plan to take him for his annual exam. The annual exam is a time for an independent eye

to evaluate his health and a time for you to ask questions. Because most illnesses in companion birds are due to diet, reviewing your conure's diet with your veterinarian and reviewing the condition of your bird on that diet is an excellent investment.

What Happens at a Well-Bird Examination?

If you haven't visited an avian veterinarian before, it will be helpful to understand the process beforehand. Additionally, if you have children, you should explain this process to your child so that she also will understand what happens during the exam. A history, observation, physical exam, and grooming will generally take place during each well-bird visit. Diagnostic tests are usually done the first time that your conure visits the vet and only when needed thereafter.

History

Your veterinarian will ask you the age and sex of your conure, where you got him, and whether your bird has had any previous medical conditions. The answers to these questions give your clinician a starting place for the examination.

If your conure's feathers are ruffled or puffed up frequently, seek veterinary attention for him.

Your vet will ask about your bird-keeping habits and procedures, the location of the cage, the amount of sleep that he gets each night, and his diet. You could bring along a sample of your conure's current diet, along with the label information from the package if it is not a diet obtained from your veterinarian.

Observation

While your bird remains in the cage, your veterinarian will observe him. Over the few minutes of history taking, your bird will relax. Trained observers notice a bird's posture on the perch, the position and condition of his feathers, whether he strains when defecating, and the rate of his breathing.

The vet also will examine the cage for signs of illness. (This is why you shouldn't change the paper at the bottom of your conure's cage before transporting him to the veterinarian.) If the cage is too large to transport, bring the paper from the bottom of the cage. Seeing your conure's feces and any regurgitated food, blood, or feathers dropped during the prior 24 hours will help your veterinarian to better understand his condition.

Physical Examination

After weighing your conure, the vet will pick him up and examine his body for fat deposits and tumors. She will check his feathers in detail, looking for

FAMILY-FRIENDLY TIP

Telling Children the Truth About an Injured or Ill Conure

Veterinarians encourage parents to be honest with their children about the health condition of their conure. Veterinarians also appreciate the opportunity to answer children's questions, as well as those of the other family members.

In most cases, children are aware of their conure's condition. A parent's overoptimistic or dismissive approach compromises the child's trust in the parent. Social workers also encourage parents to discuss the pet's true state of health using simple and clear words. "Our bird may die from this illness," is an example of a clear communication. The Delta Society (www.deltasociety.org) provides links to programs that help families who lose their pets to accident or illness.

Pets give us an opportunity to discuss death as a natural part of life with our children. An open discussion honors your conure's family membership.

parasites such as feather lice. She will examine his mouth, probably with a special light, looking for color and the absence of mucus. She will gently extend your conure's wings, one at a time, and flex them to see condition and that they move freely. She will examine his legs and feet, checking the condition of skin and nails. She will use a light to examine his eyes and ears for the presence of blood, mucus, or other discharge.

Diagnostic Tests

Based on the physical findings, your vet may suggest diagnostic tests. At your first visit, you need to have a basic blood count and a fecal test for parasites. Your vet also may suggest screening tests to ensure that the conure you purchased is free from a few of the more common incurable viral diseases.

Grooming

Have your veterinarian trim flight feathers and nails. If your new bird is an older bird, ask your vet to assess the condition of his beak and whether it needs a trim. Some older birds without proper care have overgrown beaks that can affect their ability to eat.

Having grooming done at the veterinarian's office costs no more than with a groomer at a local pet shop. Further, the technique that you observe is a proper one. If you are interested in learning about the process, ask your

Senior Bird Health

Dr. Greg Burkett describes geriatrics as the branch of avian medicine that treats problems particular to old age. Old age is not a disease. However, the aging process creates problems such as cataracts, muscle wasting, skin changes, joint stiffness, and reproductive changes.

Senior birds should be checked for skin and feather quality, as well as body condition. Of particular concern are the feet. Thinning of skin on the feet can result in foot sores and possible infections. Another serious concern is muscle wasting due to decreased level of exercise. If either of these conditions is present, your vet will discuss lifestyle and husbandry changes to try to support your senior conure.

Organ failure is a common age-related problem, with the liver and kidneys being the organs of most concern. Blood chemistry tests can detect these problems early and aid in treatment. Changes in heart rhythm and strength also occur with age. Lungs can lose function, as well. Eyes are prone to cataracts and other conditions that reduce visual capabilities.

With age, the immune system weakens and is less able to fight off certain types of bacteria. Burkett recommends annual cultures to develop an understanding of what bacteria are normal for your individual conure.

vet to help you learn to do the trims yourself.

Discuss with your vet that your goal for the wing trim is a gentle, descending flight. Likely, your vet will trim conservatively and ask you to bring your bird back if you find that the trim is not enough.

Signs That Your Conure Needs a Vet

Only one or two generations from their natural homes, conures retain all the traits of their wild relatives. In the wild, animals that look sick are targets for predators, so your companion conure will not show illness or injury until he is unable to conceal it. By the time you notice something wrong, your bird is probably very ill. Seek veterinary attention as soon as you notice signs of illness.

Indicators that something is wrong include continuously ruffled feathers, changes in potty habits, changes in the way your bird sits on the perch (e.g., favoring one foot, adopting a strange posture, etc.), and refusing to eat.

Daily Health Monitoring

You can learn to discover problems at an earlier stage by making observations a part of your bird's daily care. As you clean the cage, notice these things:
- Are the droppings normal?
- Are there any feathers or blood on the floor?

- Are your conure's activity and vocalizations normal?
- Is he standing on the perch normally?
- Is your conure eating and drinking normally?

If any points are not completely normal, look closer. Look for these changes in appearance:
- change in droppings
- drooping wings
- feathers fluffed
- food regurgitated or stuck to face
- runny eyes or nose
- weight loss

Think about whether there has been a change in behavior of these sorts:
- frequent sleeping
- labored breathing
- limping
- listlessness
- loss of appetite
- not talking, singing, or chattering

If you recognize any of these signs, contact your veterinarian immediately for a same-day appointment. Most veterinarians will find a way to admit a very sick bird who has been under their care for routine physicals, even if the schedule is booked. If your veterinarian cannot see your bird, ask for a referral to someone who can.

Whenever a bird seems ill, you must act quickly. A bird laboring to breathe in the morning will probably not be alive when you return from work.

Weight

An early sign of illness in birds is weight loss. As you remove your conure from the cage to do your cage cleaning, place him on a scale equipped with a perch. (You also can use a postal scale.) Record his weight. It takes just a moment. Keeping a weight chart is an excellent way to involve kids in bird care.

Attitude on the Perch

Before opening your companion's cage, observe how he stands on the perch. Is he standing normally or squatted low on the perch? Is he standing on the bottom of the cage or leaning against the bars? Are his feathers flat against his body, or are they elevated, giving him a fluffy appearance?

A conure who has trouble standing needs immediate veterinary attention. Later in the day may be too late. Feathers close to the body are the normal posture, while feathers elevated mean that your bird is warming his body. Constantly elevated feathers indicate that your parrot is having trouble maintaining his body temperature. Again, if you've seen this posture for more than

half an hour at normal room temperature, call your veterinarian.

Wastes

Your conure's waste is a window into his digestion and overall health. Noticing the waste each day is a good way to learn what's normal. A bird's waste comprises three parts: the liquid part of urine, the feces, and the urates (solid particles from urine, normally white). Birds release these wastes simultaneously through the cloaca (sometimes called the vent) located at the underside of the tail.

Normal Feces

Diet and stress levels provoke normal variations in your bird's poop. He excretes waste products after

Learn your conure's normal appearance and behavior so that you will notice any changes that may indicate a health problem.

digestion. Based on what you feed your bird and what his system requires, the waste looks different.

Feces (stool) are the solid wastes. Normally tube-shaped coils, their color and consistency vary. All-seed diets produce dark green to nearly black feces. Healthy formulated diet pellets yield a brown stool. Beets, pomegranates, cherries, carrots, sweet potatoes, blueberries, and squash are healthy foods that color normal feces. Colored pellets also can color feces. Remember this, and don't panic if your bird has red droppings after eating beets.

Urine, the liquid portion of your bird's excretion, always should be clear. Diets high in fruits and vegetables produce more urine.

Uric acid (urates) is the chalklike substance on top of and around the feces. The urates should always be whitish beige in color. A different color often indicates a serious problem.

Abnormal Feces: the Early Warning System

Once you know the normal appearance of your bird's droppings, you will be able to notice problems. A change in the appearance, color, or quantity of droppings is one of the earliest signs—and may be the only sign—of a sick bird.

Most veterinarians suggest newsprint or plain white paper toweling instead of shavings or other artificial bedding

How Do I Know My Conure Is Geriataric?

Green-cheeked and sun conures over the age of 18 are considered geriatric because their life expectancy is about 25 years. Assessments of the life spans of other conures are rare, as are studies of senior parrots in general.

One study, done on senior macaws from Parrot Jungle (Miami, FL), showed that thickening of the skin of the feet and appearance of warts and cataracts were frequent occurrences. Also, the parrots' postures changed due to arthritis and aging nervous systems.

Causes of death at Parrot Jungle tended to be tumors, kidney failure, and other degenerative diseases. These well-nourished parrots aged normally and did not, as many companion parrots do, suffer from conditions caused by a poor diet. Until further studies show us otherwise, we can assume that our aging conures face similar problems.

What Abnormal Droppings Can Mean

Bloody feces (red or black)	Intestinal irritation, egg binding, tumors, poisons
Brown or red urates	Lead or zinc poisoning, liver disease
Diarrhea	Sudden diet change, parasites, ingestion of foreign object
Less feces	Appetite loss, shortage of food, intestinal obstruction
More feces	Egg laying, poor digestion
Less urine	Dehydration
More urine	Normal with stress, high fruit and vegetable diet; abnormal with infectious diseases, poisons, drug reactions
Green or yellow urates	Liver disease, anorexia
Undigested food	Poor nutrition, infection, oil ingestion

because it interferes with evaluating the droppings for signs of health problems. Signs of trouble include a change in the color and amounts of urine and feces and a change in the color of the urates. Diarrhea in birds is not simply more liquid in the droppings but rather a lack of the normal tubular formation of the feces.

Common Accidents and First Aid

Although you hope that an accident will never occur, being prepared gives you and your companion the best chance of getting through an accident with the best outcome. Being aware of the frequent kinds of potential accidents gives you a way to prevent them. Knowing what to do in case of an accident is the next step. With a first-aid kit and an emergency procedure down pat, you're as prepared as you can be

and able to focus on enjoying time with your bird.

Common Accidents

Accidents cause trauma, an assault on your bird's body in a way that causes injury or death. Regular sources of trauma for companion conures include members of their human family and common household fixtures.

Companion birds allowed to roam frequently suffer crushing when a family member steps on them or rolls onto them in bed. Reclining mechanical chairs can kill birds who have crawled inside the mechanism for a dark, private place to perch.

Drowning is a frequent cause of death that occurs in places that you might never imagine. When birds fall into water, their feathers become soaked. Too heavy to climb to safety,

Feeling Good

they drown. Stovetop pots, bowls of soaking vegetables, dishes soaking in the sink, open toilet bowls, and even glasses of water have been the scene of unhappy ends.

A third type of accident occurs when a flying bird strikes a window, mirror, or ceiling fan.

A flying conure can easily get into trouble: landing on the stove, crashing into a ceiling fan, falling in the toilet bowl.

Other accidents involve burns. Birds chew electrical cords and land on stovetops and ovens more often than you'd imagine.

Finally, whether through attack or play, companion parrots can be injured or killed by other family pets, including dogs, cats, and exotics such as ferrets or snakes.

Most accidents can be averted by close supervision when your bird is out of his cage. If your conure is allowed to roam free in a room, you must do your best to bird-proof it first. Cages not only protect your household from the bird; they also protect your bird from the household.

First Aid

The goal of first aid is to stabilize your injured or ill bird so that transport to the veterinarian does not compound his problems. First aid is a prelude to, not a substitute for, veterinary care.

Levels of Priority

Severe bleeding or blood flowing from a wound must be stopped immediately, even before calling your veterinarian. This is a life-threatening emergency.

Nonlife-threatening illnesses or injuries cause distress and pain. These include fractures, diarrhea, or vomiting. The goal is to prevent the injury or illness from worsening and prepare the bird for transport to your vet.

Minor injuries include superficial abrasions. You can care for your bird at home if you know how and take him to the vet if the injury does not improve.

Bleeding and Broken Bones

If your bird has obvious bone breaks or bleeding of any kind, stop the bleeding and stabilize the fracture. Capture your bird with a pillowcase or sheet. Use the pillowcase or a large paper towel to restrain him to prevent further injury and allow examination. Use the penlight from your first-aid kit to get a good look at the affected area.

To stop bleeding, use gentle pressure on the wound with sterile gauze. If the bleeding is from a blood feather, use styptic powder to stop the bleeding in the broken feather shaft. If you don't have styptic powder, flour or cornstarch will work.

To stabilize fractures, restrain your conure's motion. Think tubular: a sock or panty hose leg with the toe cut out. Ensure that your bird is not wrapped so tightly that he cannot breathe or that he overheats. Consider the outside temperature, the temperature of your bird, and the distance to your veterinarian. Alternative restraints include your first-aid kit stocking or a paper towel over the wings held in place with masking tape.

Animal Bites

Bites from animals can be life-threatening emergencies. Not only can there be obvious or hidden puncture wounds from a bite, but there can be internal injuries and fractures resulting from the crush of the animal's jaws. In addition, infections develop from bites and scratches. The first 24 hours after the bite are critical. Even if your bird appears bright and alert, take him to your veterinarian immediately. As

always, stopping any bleeding is your first priority.

Bleeding From a Broken Nail or Beak

Catch your conure and apply direct pressure to the injury using a towel or your finger. If a minute or two of pressure doesn't stop the bleeding, apply styptic powder, cornstarch, or flour. Observe the bird for an hour after the bleeding stops. If a piece of nail or beak is cracked or dangling, it needs to be removed. Call your vet right away for further instructions.

What to Do When an Accident Befalls Your Conure

1. Take a deep breath to calm yourself.
2. Remove your bird from the threatening situation.
3. Get your first-aid kit and administer vital first aid.
4. Call your veterinarian before leaving home.
5. Say "This is an emergency," as your first words to the receptionist.
6. In one sentence, explain the problem. ("My conure has been stepped on," or "My conure is having trouble breathing," or "My bird is fluffed and needs to be seen right away.")
8. Ask for advice before transporting.

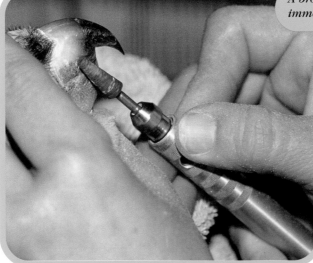

ken, so support the wing as you pull out the feather. After removal, apply pressure directly on the follicle for one to two minutes using a cotton ball or gauze. Once you have controlled the bleeding, observe your bird for an hour because bleeding can recur.

Bleeding From a Broken Blood Feather

Sometimes birds break feathers before the feather is fully developed. Developing feathers have an active blood supply. When these feathers break, blood drips without stopping because the "vein" has been opened. To stop the bleeding, you may have to remove the feather shaft from the follicle, where it attaches to the wing. This requires two people, one to restrain the bird and one to remove the feather.

Call your veterinarian for coaching on how to do this. If you cannot find help, restrain your bird and pull out the feather without delay. Use sturdy tweezers or needle-nosed pliers to grasp the feather as close to the skin as possible. Bird bones are easily bro-

Fractures

Fractures are painful, but they are also a sign that your bird could have more serious injuries from the trauma that caused the fracture. Pet birds fracture legs more commonly than they fracture wings. Signs of leg fractures include the bird refusing to stand on the leg or the leg hanging in an awkward position. A fractured wing will hang lower than the other, and the bird will be unable to move his wing.

With fractures, confine the bird to a small carrier padded with a towel. Keep him warm. If possible, immobilize the wing by binding it to the body, either with a stocking with a hole cut in the toe or with a towel draped like a cape, encircled with masking tape. For a fractured leg, immobilize it by wrapping it onto a tongue depressor cut to the correct length or another flat, rigid object.

Oiled Feathers

Unbelievably, birds frequently fall into tubs with bath oil or pans of oil in the garage. Birds lose their ability to regulate their temperature when feathers are oiled, so it's crucial that you contact your veterinarian as soon as you discover the situation. Cleaning an oil-soaked bird requires multiple steps, best done by an experienced person.

If you cannot reach your veterinarian, dust oiled feathers with cornstarch or flour to soak up the excess oil. (Be sure to keep your bird's eyes and nose clear.) Wrap him in a towel to reduce heat loss and to prevent him from trying to remove the oil himself. (Ingested oil could be fatal.) After 30 minutes, fill a sink with warm water and add a minute amount of dishwashing soap. (Dawn is recommended.) Wet all affected feathers by handling them gently and following the contours. Dip the bird slowly for one or two minutes. Rinse the feathers well with fresh, warm water. Repeat as needed. Blot feathers dry.

Capturing and Restraining Your Conure

When an accident happens, the first thing to do is to capture and safely restrain your bird. With a panicked conure, the easiest way to do this is with a towel. If you are not accustomed to handling your conure, taking hold can be the most stressful part of the process for you and him. Have what you need ready before starting, and work quickly.

Drape the towel over your hand. Grasp either side of your conure's head with your towel-draped thumb and forefinger, keeping in mind that bird bones are fragile. Place your index finger over the top of his head for security. Lift the bird, supporting his body with your other hand.

Wrap the loose ends of the towel around his wings and feet. When toweling is complete, your conure should be secure in the towel, able to inhale and exhale easily.

Sometimes conures are so distressed that immobilizing them is difficult. In these cases, consider dropping a sheet or pillowcase over your conure to stop his terrorized fleeing. Gain control of his head by bringing your thumb and forefinger around the base of his skull so that he doesn't bite you. Use your other hand to immobilize his wings by grasping them gently through the sheet. If no other help is available, raise him until you can secure his wings with slight pressure of your arm against your body.

Place a cardboard box so that half of it is on a heating pad set on low and half of it is off the heating pad. Heat until the temperature in the cardboard box reaches 85°F (29.4°C). Monitor the temperature of the box very carefully so as not to overheat your conure. The box should remain at this temperature until he is dry. Steps may need to be repeated several times for thorough cleaning.

Poisoning

A poisoned bird may suddenly regurgitate, develop diarrhea, go into convulsions, or show signs of redness or burns around his mouth or his body. Birds can be poisoned by inhaling fumes, eating a poisonous plant or chemical, or coming into contact with poison on the skin. If your bird is overcome by fumes, open all the windows and move him into fresh air.

The most common cause of inhaled poisoning is the coating on nonstick cookware, so conure companions should get rid of any nonstick cookware in the house. The Teflon coating on some space heaters can also cause poisoning.

If the poison is a contact poison, flush the skin with water. Call your veterinarian and ask to be seen immediately. Bring the poison in the original container with you, if possible.

If you are unable to reach your veterinarian, call the ASPCA Animal Poison Control Center hotline at 888-426-4435. Have a credit card ready. The

Transport Your Bird Safely

When an emergency occurs, you must take your bird to the vet's office as soon as possible. Call your veterinarian before leaving home and explain the emergency so that her office is ready for your arrival. This saves time. Either the staff can prepare to treat your bird immediately, or they can direct you to a place that can.

Have someone else drive so that you can comfort and watch your bird. If this is not possible, place your confined bird in the back seat of your car on the passenger side so that you can see each other. Stay calm and drive carefully. Unless the day is sweltering, use a hot water bottle to supply warmth. Fill a dishwashing glove with hot water, and close it with a rubber band as a substitute hot water bottle.

If the cage is small, leave your bird in it, cover it to keep him calm and warm, and transport him without delay. If the cage is large and cannot be taken into the veterinarian's office, you must catch and restrain your bird for transport in a travel cage.

First Aid Kit Contents

Item	Use
Veterinarian and closest emergency care hospital telephone number, address, and directions	Saves time, eliminates confusion
Small pad and pencil	Make notes about your bird's condition before calling vet; write down the vet's instructions
Towel and pillowcase	Catching and restraining your bird
Styptic powder, flour, cornstarch	To stop bleeding of broken blood feather or toenail
Gauze roll, gauze squares, vet wrap, half-inch (1.3 cm) masking tape, scissors	Wound dressing to stop bleeding for transport
Apple juice, powdered Gatorade, eye dropper	Quick energy source
Heating pad and hot water bottle	Sources of heat
Penlight	Light source
Tweezers, needle-nosed pliers	Remove blood feather
Hydrogen peroxide and cotton swabs	Antiseptic to clean wounds
Eye irrigation solution (saline)	Flush wounds and eyes
Box or container	Keep items together for home or travel
Nail clipper, nail file	Clip and smooth overgrown nails

charge is a flat fee, and making the call gives your bird a chance to survive.

Common Illnesses

Other bird emergencies result from disease. Birds are masters at disguising illness, even from their experienced human companions. This genetic programming helps wild birds to evade predators that watch for slow-moving prey to attack.

If a pet bird keeps his feathers fluffed, acts weak, coughs, has nasal discharge or diarrhea, fails to eat, sleeps more than usual, limps, or has swellings or sores, he requires immediate veterinary attention. Call your vet within minutes, not hours or days.

If the cage is small enough, take the entire cage. It may hold clues to your bird's illness. If not, take the paper from the bottom of the cage with droppings or regurgitated material for your vet to examine. Droppings or other material can provide clues about the origin of your bird's illness when examined by a vet.

Avian Illness in the Media

Even though West Nile virus (WNV) and the bird flu are frequently mentioned in the media, these diseases pose little threat for companion birds. For conures who stay indoors, almost no threat exists.

Because only mosquitoes transmit West Nile virus, the trick is to eliminate your conure's exposure to these insects. Keeping screens closed and taking your bird inside at early morning and dusk, when mosquitoes are active, provides the most practical protection. In areas where WNV is present, less than 1 percent of mosquitoes carry the virus, so the chance of your conure being infected is low. Even when wild birds in your area die from the disease, pet birds can be protected by excluding mosquitoes. Be cautious about mosquito control with insecticide use, though. Insecticides are poisons, and birds have sensitive respiratory systems.

For conure owners, vaccination for WNV is neither practical nor necessary. Although a vaccine is commonly used on horses, the physiology and disease course is different in birds. Check your bird protection plan with your veterinarian.

Bird flu transmission occurs through contact with feces from sick birds. Keeping your conure isolated from the feces of wild birds should be sufficient protection. This preventive measure also eliminates the transmission of many more common and likely diseases.

Diseases that can be seen in conures include aspergillosis, chlamydiosis (also called psittacosis), and Pacheco's disease.

Aspergillosis

Aspergillosis is the most frequent respiratory and fungal disease in pet birds. The fungus grows on moldy cage litter, grain, and peanut shells. This disease is rarely seen in birds who eat a formulated diet. Birds sickened by aspergillosis are lethargic, their lungs are congested, and their appetite is suppressed. Veterinarians treat this illness with one of several antifungal agents, sometimes for as long as four to six months. Special care is needed, including keeping the parrot warm, fluid therapy, and unique nutritional support. Usually, you can prevent this illness by keeping the cage and surroundings clean, feeding only fresh seeds and grains, and only feeding shelled peanuts.

Chlamydiosis

Chlamydiosis is caused by bacteria that live in people as well as in parrots. For this reason, chlamydiosis is a public health concern.

Associated with flu-like symptoms in people, avian signs include eye or nasal discharge, a lack of interest in food, bright green urates, and diarrhea. Requiring significant testing to confirm a diagnosis, avian psittacosis treatment is usually based on the antibiotic doxycycline, which is given for 45 days.

Pacheco's Disease

Pacheco's disease is caused by a virus. Clinical signs can be very slight and include depression, failure to eat, and a lethargic attitude. Infrequently, regurgitation and bloody diarrhea are reported as signs. This disease underlines the dictum that with birds, if

Have your bird carrier set up and waiting, so you'll be ready if an emergency happens.

they don't look right on the perch, take them to the veterinarian immediately. As masters of disease disguise, birds are often quite sick before they show signs.

Veterinarians can prescribe antiviral agents for birds with Pacheco's disease. A vaccine has been developed as well. Discuss with your veterinarian whether a vaccination is advisable for your bird.

Mites

Mites are a skin and feather parasite that result in the thickening and flaking of skin. Mites can cause inflammation of the face and the cere, the location of the bird's nostrils. Your veterinarian can treat mites with injections, an oral medication, or both.

Feeling Good

Chapter 6

Being Good

Conures are individuals. No book can teach you how to handle your conure in your specific situation. Quiet, patient observation and experimentation are the best teachers. Although we speak about training as if it is about your parrot, training is about both parrot and person. Training is learning to communicate, and it is a way to develop a relationship that will last a lifetime. It is also a way to get past the difficult times. If your conure is well trained, and if you are conditioned to ask for and reward behaviors from your bird, the training will supersede the daily ups and downs in your emotional and physical states.

I n human relationships, unfailing courtesy is often cited as what keeps marriages together for 30 or 40 years. You might think of continuous consistent asking for and rewarding of behaviors in conures as a form of unfailing courtesy. Each of you knows what is being asked and what is expected. This is the basis for success.

Benefits and Approach to Training

Each time that you interact with your conure, either you are training your bird or your bird is training you. Training is a state of mind—you ask your bird to do something, she does it, and you reward her. You won't believe the fun that you and your parrot will have!

Benefits

The benefits of doing some training with your new conure are enormous. What you want is a companion whom you can easily move around your home, bring in and out of his cage, and have pleasant day-to-day interactions with as you go about his care and providing him with companionship.

Other reasons to work on training daily include:
- to maintain the sweetness of your young bird

Take a Time Out

When you're feeling rushed, curtail your interaction with your bird. Better, set the timer for 15 minutes and spend that time observing and talking with your bird. Wait until you're relaxed to pick up your conure.

- to build on the good aspects of an older bird's behavior
- to keep your bird mentally stimulated
- to vary your bird's daily routine
- to have a way to handle your bird in stressful circumstances

Approach

If birds are new to you, you must develop the skill of thinking like one. Avoiding behavior problems and

Training is a way to develop a lifelong relationship with your conure.

Positive, reward-based training results in a happy and satisfying conure-companion relationship.

encouraging good behavior is the best way forward. Conures are not like dogs; they don't care whether they please you or not—they want what they want. The trick is understanding what your conure wants and using that to your advantage. Think about bird handling as a game of tactics.

You must realize that punishment is never a part of training your conure. You can't spank a bird. You can't make him feel ashamed. Terrifying your conure will multiply his behavior problems exponentially.

Establish Routines

Talk or sing to your conure before you turn out the light or cover the cage at night. Use the same phrase every night. Like children who find comfort in nursery rhymes, conures like repetition. When you leave the house, say "Bye bye." When you return, go over to the cage immediately and say "Hello." Spend a few minutes before you sit down to rest to talk with your parrot. When you do cage maintenance, tell him what you are doing. Your conure does not understand what you're saying. What he does understand is that you're focused on him, and that's the point.

It is important to work with your conure every day. Parrots are creatures of habit, and training one is a slow, gradual task. They respond to every interaction with you, so keep your interactions positive. The benefit to you is your strengthening relationship as you move forward.

Use Positive Reinforcement

Positive reinforcement means praising the bird immediately when you see the behavior that you want and ignoring behavior that you don't want. To highlight the desired behavior, create what behaviorists call a bridge. "Good job" is a common bridge. The first part of the training is to establish the bridge. In other words, your bird needs to associate the words "good job" with a reward, which is a tiny treat. You need this because you cannot always get the treat to the bird fast enough to let him know which of the various behaviors he did that is being rewarded. Be consistent, and always offer the reward for the desired behavior.

Train in a Neutral Place

A neutral place is a quiet room where just you and your bird can focus on each other, without a cage, television, or other pets to distract your session. Normally, a T-stand, a stick, and some favorite treats are all the equipment you need.

Keep training sessions short at first—five minutes or so. Be sure to stop on a positive experience. You may train two or three times each day.

Necessary Training: the Basic Two

There are many behaviors you might want to train your bird to do. It is probably best to start with simple ones and build up to behaviors that are more complex. The following two behaviors are simple and useful and will establish a foundation for further training.

Stick Training

Stick training is the first step toward establishing good bird citizenry. Having your conure step willingly onto a stick that you present is important. When your bird is frightened or injured but needs to be moved, a stick is one way to accomplish this without your being bitten. Alternatively, if someone unfamiliar to your bird needs to move him, the stick allows that person to work with your bird with confidence.

With stick training, as with any training, the best approach is to move your bird to a neutral space, one located away from the cage he considers home. Often a bathroom or guest room is a good quiet space. Set up a T-stand and have your conure perch and settle on the stand.

Keep a pile of small but favored treats, such as half a pine nut or a tiny piece of sunflower seed meat, within your reach but outside your conure's

It is important for your conure to learn to step up onto your hand and a stick.

reach (for example, in a pocket). Most birds will work for food. If your bird will not work for food, you haven't selected something appealing enough.

For stick training, your goals are to acclimate your bird to the stick and to entice him to stand on it. Holding the stick in one hand by your side, give your bird a treat. Say "Good job." Feed a treat. Move the stick closer. If your conure remains relaxed, say "Good job." Feed another treat. Show your conure the stick. Say "Good job." Feed another treat. If your conure shows any concern about the stick, continue to work with the stick, but keep it away from your bird until he relaxes. Depending on his experience with sticks, he may be relaxed from the beginning, or he may take weeks to relax.

When your conure shows no concern about the stick, place it slightly higher than the T-stand and have him stretch toward the stick to claim his treat. Always say "Good job" before you give the treat, and always have your bird work a little harder for the next treat. Keep the stick higher than the T-stand, because parrots want to step higher, not lower. Continue moving the treat back each time until your conure must step onto the stick to take the treat.

Once your conure has done this, place the stick lower than the T-stand and have him step onto the T-stand. Say "Good job." Give him the treat.

At this stage, reinforce the behavior

Treats for Training

Training treats should be as small as possible but still be an incentive. Examples include portions of a hulled seed or nut, such as half a sunflower seed, a slice of pine nut, or a crumble of pecan meat. Birds fill up quickly, so small treats keep the motivation going. In addition, your conure can eat small treats quickly. Small treats equal more training time.

for one or two sessions. For future sessions, present the stick and say "Step up." When he steps onto the stick, say "Good job." Give him the treat.

Step Up

The second aspect of good bird citizenry is for your bird to step onto your hand when asked. Train this behavior using the T-stand, but then reinforce it outside of your training sessions.

As you train your bird to step onto your hand, you want him to step off

Once you have the basics of training down, you can teach your conure to do many fun tricks.

trained your conure, this training should be easier. The goal is that when you say "Up," no matter where your bird is, he should raise his foot to step onto your hand or the offered stick.

The tricky part of this exercise is to have your bird willingly leave your hand. I use the command "Down." In the beginning, you can have him step onto your hand, step onto the stick, and then step down. Leaving the stick is usually easier than leaving the preferred person's hand.

Use the same principles as before. Hold training sessions for five minutes or less several times each day. Treat with the preferred food every time until the behavior is established, and then gradually reduce to an occasional treat for compliance.

At the T-stand, place your hand and index and third fingers parallel to the ground and parallel to the T-stand crossbar, at the base of your conure's chest. Say "Up." Touch your conure's chest with your extended fingers. Most birds will step onto your hand willingly. Say "Good job." Treat.

Most birds require very few sessions to learn these commands. Be consistent. Work a few minutes each time, and always end on a successful note.

Socialization

Socialization means that a bird learns the life skills necessary to be a companion parrot. This includes

easily. When he steps on and off your hand easily, you then want him to step onto and off a stick. Having stick

Acclimating Your Conure to a Carrier

Having a conure who is willing and eager to enter his carrier is a convenience that you'll be grateful for the first time you need to rush to the veterinarian's office.

One way to ensure that your bird willingly enters his carrier is to make every carrier entry experience a good one.

Some human companions feed their conures inside the carrier. Not only does this create a relaxed atmosphere for the bird, but it makes messy fruit cleanup easier for the companion.

Other companions use the travel cage as the sleeping cage. Again, if you have a nighttime ritual that involves moving your bird to his travel cage, by giving him a good-night treat and scratching his ears, he will come to associate the carrier with very good things.

If your carrier is used only as a carrier, you will need to train your conure to enter it and stay calm once inside. Start by rewarding him for going toward the enclosure. Once he understands this, reward him for touching the carrier. Next, reward him for going inside. By doing this gradually, your conure will eventually enter and remain in the carrier eagerly, knowing he will be rewarded.

learning about food, language, and acceptable behavior.

Young parrots are socialized by their parents and their flock. Because you are (or should be) the leader of your bird's flock, it is up to you to teach your bird life skills. Well-socialized companion birds lead full lives because they can travel by car, willingly go to a variety of people, eat a variety of foods, are pleasant during cage maintenance, and are fun at playtime.

Whatever your parrot's level of socialization, just move forward. Each bird's experience has been different. Your life together will benefit if you accept your bird as he is but provide the opportunity for both of you to improve.

Cage-Bound Birds

If your bird does not come out of his cage, try:

1. Ambient attention: Sit near the cage

while you read aloud to your kids or watch television. When the bird shows interest, repeat the phrase or sound that stimulated your bird.

2. Hand feed: Spend five minutes each day offering a variety of favored foods. If all else fails, try feeding millet. Talk with your bird using a quiet, calm voice.

Lack of Confidence

If your bird comes out of the cage but you're not confident with each other, try these activities:

1. Take your bird on a tour of a different room of your house each day, pointing out interesting sights including mirrors, pictures, and windows.
2. Perch your bird nearby while you work on a project such as peeling vegetables, sewing, or working on the computer.
3. If your goal is to go outside, start by feeding your bird in his travel cage. After he is comfortable eating in the small cage, take a sandwich and your crated bird and head to your balcony or patio. (Remember, birds must be caged or harnessed outdoors to be safe.)

One-Person Birds

Parrots are flock animals, and they learn through imitation. Give your parrot the message that everyone in your home is safe.

Have someone else actually deliver the food to your bird's cage. Hand your bird to others as often as possible. Give the new or less-favored person your bird's favorite toy or a treat to occupy him. Additional activities include:

1. Pass your bird to a friend. Take him back. Pass him to another friend. Let him learn that he's safe in the hands of friends.
2. When you go out for the evening or travel overnight, take your conure in a carrier. He will become used to new people and the car. Ensure that your bird is comfortable with the carrier first, and always reward good behavior.

As you try these activities, watch your parrot's appearance. The position

Hand feeding can speed up the socialization process.

of his feathers, his body posture, and his vocalization indicate his state of mind. When he's anxious, slow down or take a step back.

Talking

Enthusiasm and energy are the keys to getting conures to talk. Teaching new phrases is an activity children enjoy. Remember that not every conure will talk, and keep in mind that different conures have varying levels of skill when it comes to talking and mimicry.

To teach your bird to talk, first decide on a phrase. Repeat it several times. When your bird tries to repeat the phrase, give the bridge words "Good job" and offer a reward. Teach one phrase until your bird continually tries to use it. Then move to the next.

Talking birds are charming until they aren't. Most bird guardians have experienced the humiliation of a super-sized "breaking wind" sound followed by maniacal laughter or a singsong "Oh shoot!" as background for a business telephone call. If you react with shouting or laughter, you will encourage your bird to repeat the unwanted sound or phrase. It is better to ignore it and reward some other behavior.

Natural Behaviors That Are Sometimes Problems

When your bird exhibits a behavior that's a problem for you, take a few minutes to consider why he is performing this behavior—what does he get out of it? If you know why your bird is doing a problem behavior, your chances of correcting it improve. The secret to preventing problem behaviors is to preempt them—stop them before they start. The key to coping with problem behaviors is not to obsess about them but to treat them as a part of daily life, having decided in advance what you will and will not do in response.

Parrots have nothing to do but bend you to their will unless you give them important jobs to do. On average, wild parrots spend 50 percent of their

97

FAMILY-FRIENDLY TIP

Conure Tricks for Kids

Three good tricks for children to start with are "turn around," "wave," and "shake hands." "Turn around" is an especially good one. The website www.parrottricks.com has printable instructions for training these simple tricks. Video versions of the training instructions are also available for download. Kids can learn handling skills from the videos, and the bird gets to spend busy time with his flockmates.

Being Good

waking hours looking for and eating food, 25 percent of the time interacting with a mate or other flock members, and 25 percent preening. Most problem behaviors arise either because a bird does not have enough to do, because the bird is getting insufficient exercise, or both.

Biting

When your conure is fearful, he will bite. Fear often arises when a bird is approached too quickly or confronted with something new without time to acclimate. Aggressive biting can occur when your conure becomes overloaded with excitement. A bird who has been battering a toy does not calm down when you put your hand up to remove him from the play stand. He bites in a continuation of the roughhousing he started with the toy. Another reason for biting is that your conure learns that he can avoid what he doesn't want to do by biting.

When your bird exhibits fear or aggression, avoid handling him at that moment. If you must handle him, use the stick he's been trained to climb onto, or use a towel to gently move him.

When they're not getting enough time out of the cage, many birds refuse to go back in. Also, when you give the "down" command and expect your normally compliant bird to leave your hand for his perch, he

may nip or bite. If you know that this is going to be an issue, preempt the problem and put him on the stick at a point when he's compliant. Use the stick to transfer him to the cage. Offer the treat so that your bird must step off the stick but can take the treat with his tongue through the bars.

Many birds going through adolescence can be aggressive. If your bird is going through an aggressive period, use the stick instead of your hand as the vehicle of transport.

Successful bird handling requires that you understand your bird's state of mind and use the technique that will work on that day to preserve the trusting relationship that you have. Like people, birds have their good days and

Repetition and enthusiasm are the keys to getting your conure to talk.

their bad days. When you're in a bad mood and your bird is in a bad mood, no handling is the best plan. If handling is necessary to do cage cleaning on one of these days, use the stick.

Screaming

Birds in a flock stay in touch by calling to one another. As a part of a flock, you have an obligation to answer or your flockmate will call, louder and louder, until you answer. The volume you use to answer is related to the volume that the bird becomes accustomed to using.

Screaming is a behavior that increases the energy and drama in the household. Many conure species are known to scream, especially between early light and midmorning, and during the twilight hours. Although some species of conure are less loud than others, just about all birds are vocally active in the morning and at night.

A typical unpleasant scene is an escalating screaming match between parrot and companion. "Hello." "Screech." "Be quiet." "Screech" in a louder voice. Each cycle of screech and response will be delivered louder than the one before. If you cannot interrupt the cycle, then ignoring the behavior that you want to eliminate is the best course. Make a note of the time so that tomorrow you will not miss the opportunity for your preemptive strike. If you play music at the screeching hour to keep company with your bird,

lowering the music can sometimes cause your screamer to lower his voice.

Aside from the morning and afternoon activity times, there are strategies that work well if your bird's calls are very loud. These alternative strategies include whispering, a cage cover, and providing food that takes quite a while to eat. Quality and shape of the food, rather than quantity, can speed or slow eating, digestion, and elimination.

Energy ripples through a flock. If you are hyperactive, nervous, or yelling, your bird will amp up his energy and his volume. If you are quiet and attentive, you'll find that your bird is more likely to be, too. Breathe deeply and quiet yourself before you answer your bird or pick him up. A well-behaved bird will be your reward. If your bird's calls pierce your ears, try answering in a very soft voice. Whisper to him when you talk to him; he will learn to whisper to you in return.

Keep in mind that if you choose one of the louder conures, you should expect your bird to call loudly for many minutes twice each day. No amount of strategy will make that stop. It's what the louder conures do. Also, remember that a conure who is well socialized, gets plenty of attention, and has plenty to do is less likely to scream frequently.

Chewing

Chewing on wood is normal for your conure—this is not a behavior problem. To protect your treasured objects, simply keep him away from them. Ask yourself how many blocks of pine you need this week to keep your bird whittling happily.

Feather chewing and chewing on fingers are entirely different behaviors. Feather chewing should precipitate a visit to the veterinarian. Chewing on fingers is a case of putting your fingers where they should not be. Finger chewing is a stage that young birds go through. From the beginning, teach your bird that chewing toys is fine, but chewing fingers is not okay.

If you are not diligent in giving your bird a toy when he wants to chew something, the bites will become harder, and what was once an amusing game with a baby parrot will become a painful game with an adolescent bird. Improper handling of this situation has caused many conures to lose their homes.

Solving Behavior Problems

It may be difficult to see, but the root of conure behavior problems is almost always the conure's human companion. Guess who taught the bird the bad words and the bad behavior? That's right—the human in the bird's life! So how do you get your bird to stop? The best answer is to figure out how you caused the behavior in the first place.

Birds respond to energy, enthusiasm, and attention. Make a list of the words and other vocal behaviors that you don't like. For a day or two, jot down the time and what is happening

Introducing New Things

Social animals, conures learn from their flock during long "childhoods" about the safety of new things such as foods, perches, behaviors, noises, surrounding creatures, and other flock members. "Parrots see, parrots do" is another way to think about it. If a fellow flock member is eating it, bathing in it, standing on it, or playing with it, and that flock member remains alive, then it must be okay. If you want to teach your bird to bathe, for example, you're going to be dangling your fingers in the plate of water, saying "Isn't this fun?" while your parrot watches for several days. One day, your bird will get in the water because you showed him it was safe and fun. You can extend this concept to new foods, new toys, and new situations (such as the scary feather duster or the new sofa).

next to the item on the list when the word or behavior occurs. Then, strategize before you take action.

Solution 1: Ignore Bad Behavior and Encourage Good Behavior

A simple concept that you can use to change parrot behavior is to ignore unwanted behavior and praise good behavior. Using this strategy, ignore the swear word or the unseemly sound. Cue your family members to do the same. Think about it. If, when your bird screams, you shout "Bad bird! Quiet, Egore," Egore gets you, your attention, and a dramatic shouting performance as entertainment… and maybe a treat that you offer in desperation to quiet the racket. This is the bird equivalent of a movie and dessert—all for the puny cost of an earsplitting shouting session. Who's training whom?

Don't forget the second step. Praise your bird with attention or treats for saying or doing something you want. Your conure will figure how to get the desired reward and start offering the behaviors you want instead of those that get ignored.

Solution 2: Change the Vocalization to Something Acceptable

Changing bad words into good ones or loud vocalizations into softer ones is often more effective than trying to eliminate the word or sound altogether. Next time you hear an unacceptable word, react as if you do want to hear it, but change the word. Instead of

Correcting Behavior Problems

You may experience an irresistible impulse to give a "correction" to a bird. Don't. If your bird makes an undesirable word or sound, the worst approach is to shout "Bad bird." In seconds, you will have trained your bird to repeat the original bad word and then shout "Bad bird, bad bird," laughing while you rage. Your mantra should be "reward good behavior; ignore bad behavior."

"Mandy," the old girlfriend's name, you could say "Dandy. Dandy yes, I like it too!" or "candy," or any other word that sounds similar.

If the volume is the problem, try whispering. This may be contrary to how you've handled this in the past, trying to "outtalk" your bird. Whispering intrigues most birds. In fact, your conure may learn to whisper and love it.

Solution 3: Cover Up

Before your last nerve snaps, consider the cover up. Cover your bird for 10 minutes. Like an overstimulated two-year-old, your parrot may need a few minutes to lower his energy level. After a few minutes of shouting, you do, too. Make sure that the cage cover is thick and dark. Don't think of this as a punishment—it's a change of

Being Good

environment. Set a timer for ten minutes. After your timer goes off, do something interactive with your bird, finding reasons to use lots of praise.

Solution 4: Remember Perspective

Parrots in the wild communicate with flock members to ensure their safety. They are also social communicators in the morning and at dusk. Plan to spend some time talking with your conure at these times. Then, leave him plenty of uninterrupted time to play in the morning and sleep at night. If you spend more time with your companion at the time when he's active, he's less likely to try to make you active when he should be playing or asleep.

Think like a bird. Birds were engineered to communicate over long distances to their social partners. When your conure talks to you, answer. When he needs attention morning and night, give it. You'll find that he gets quieter and you become happier the more that you interact.

Squirt Bottles Are for Showers

Do not to fall prey to the concept that the squirt bottle is to punish birds vocalizing loudly. Birds need baths or showers. If you use the squirt bottle for punishment, imagine your conure's reaction when you go to bathe him!

When You Can't Solve It Yourself

Conures and human beings have different standards of behavior and methods of communication. These different standards result in frequent misunderstandings, especially at the beginning of your experience with birds. Before frustration escalates petty bickering into all-out warfare, call an avian behavioral consultant. Behavioral consultants can interpret your bird's attempt to communicate with you and can teach you to understand your bird's body language.

An avian behavioral consultant also will assist you in setting up a home environment and schedule of activities that promote avian and companion satisfaction. Some companions engage a behavioral consultant before or shortly after acquiring a bird, before trouble arises.

Most consultants work by telephone. If you prefer an in-home consultation, most consultants offer this service when the distance is not prohibitive. You can find a behavioral consultant by contacting local bird clubs, reading bird publications, and talking with local bird shops. You can also try the Internet, being sure to search on bird behavior consultants and not bird behaviorists. The first is what you need; the second is a degreed person with university research experience.

How can you determine if a behavioral consultant is right for you? Request a conversation about her experience with your type of bird and your specific problem at no charge. Ask for references. Your best consultant will have hands-on experience with both your species and the problem.

Conure Body Language

Conure body language is a "must learn" for human companions. Think about it: Without lips and other mobile facial parts or a meaningful tone of voice, birds say it all with their bodies. The trick is learning the subtleties, which is where the beak hits the skin, so to speak.

The Comfortable Conure

Comfortable conures do not perch with the vigilance of prey animals. A relaxed and confident parrot usually fluffs his feathers just enough so that he seems a bit pudgy.

Other signs of a happy, contented, or sleepy bird include preening, tail shaking, stretching, beak grinding, and standing on one foot. Conures often engage in these behaviors just prior to taking a midday nap or prior to roosting for the night.

The Aggressive or Excited Conure

Parrots show aggression with threat displays that include standing tall, spreading their wings, raising their crest or nape feathers, and swaying back and

forth. Open-beak lunging or lunge biting is very aggressive behavior.

The difference between the fluffed feathers of a relaxed bird and the erect feathers of an aggressive bird is clear if you know what to look for. Fluffed feathers blend, while erect feathers stand out individually or in groups. When aggressive, birds normally erect the feathers on the crest and the nape of the neck.

Excited birds also flash colorful parts of the body such as the wings or tail as warnings. Conures, like all parrots, rapidly contract and expand their pupils (called "pinning") when excited. Pinning the eyes is often a sign of aggression.

Excitement sometimes looks similar to aggression in parrots, but an excited parrot is more likely to be very

Giving your conure a few hours of attention each day will help prevent behavior problems from developing.

vocal. With the aggressive or excited bird, the best approach is no approach at all. Let the bird, overloaded with one stimulus or another, calm down in the same way that you would give a small child a time-out to let her emotions settle.

The Fearful Conure
Fearful conures stand stiffly, feathers flat against the body. The head may be held high, and the wings held away from the body, sometimes quivering. Repeatedly raising one foot or shifting weight is another sign of a conure

The erected feathers and spread out tail show that this blue-crowned conure is feeling aggressive.

who is frightened and confused about what to do.

It's important to discover what is causing stress for your bird and then remove or prevent these factors. If stress is being caused by something that should be normal in a companion parrot's life, then gradually introduce that thing to the parrot so that it no longer causes a negative reaction.

Considering a Companion Conure?
If you're still considering a conure as a companion, become a part of the community of conure lovers—both those who love conures in the wild and those who love conures as companion animals.

Conures fascinate with their habits, their plumage, and their gregarious natures. The fact is that the people lured into a lifelong fascination with conures fear for their safety, both as pets and as a wild species. To love a conure, you can do no better than to assure that you're making a lifelong commitment to keeping a pet who is difficult, messy, loud, and who bites. The sad fact is that many of the most alluring-looking conures spend most of their lives passing from home to home.

To repeat a point made earlier, wild, vocal, and adapted for life in the jungle, a conure can stress a family already

Conure Body Language Interpreter

Sign	Conure's Physical Action	The Conure Means
Tail wagging	Quickly wag tail back and forth	That was interesting—what's next? Also, something like a giggle.
Stretching	Shoulders raised, followed by extension of one wing and foot, usually in unison	Greeting for a person entering the room or beginning to interact with the bird.
Preening	Cleaning and zipping the feathers	I feel safe and secure.
Facial feathers fluffed	Face feathers fluffed over the beak accompanied by self-scratching	Pay attention to me, please.
Wing flipping	Slapping one wing and then the other against body	I'm frustrated.
Pinpointing or tail fan	Pupils enlarge and contract, tail feathers fan out and in	Danger. Stand back. I'm going to bite you.
Beak grinding	Rubbing lower mandible against the upper	I'm content. I'm going to sleep shortly.

leading an overcommitted life. As alluring as conures are, you have to love the work of giving a companion or pet bird an interesting life.

Whether you choose to bring a conure into your home or not, you can bring conures into your life. The World Parrot Trust and the International Conure Association (ICA) all have programs to support conures in the wild. Your lifelong fascination with birds may take you to work with these organizations or simply to provide moral or financial support for their work.

If you choose to bring a conure companion into your home, remember that you are not alone. Members of your conure support team include your veterinarian, bird behaviorists, and a large community of conure breeders and enthusiasts. If all else fails, the network of humane societies can put you in touch with experts to help.

Who wouldn't love a conure?

Resources

Organizations

American Federation of Aviculture
P.O.Box 7312
N. Kansas City, MO 64116
www.afabirds.org

Avicultural Society of America
PO Box 5516
Riverside, CA 92517-5516
www.asabirds.org

The Gabriel Foundation
1025 Acoma Street
Denver, CO 80204
www.thegabrielfoundation.org

Emergency Resources and Rescue Organizations

ASPCA Animal Poison Control Center
Telephone: (888) 426-4435
E-mail: napcc@aspca.org (for non-emergency, general information only)
www.apcc.aspca.org

Bird Hotline
P.O. Box 1411
Sedona, AZ 86339-1411
E-mail: birdhotline@birdhotline.com
www.birdhotline.com/

Bird Placement Program
P.O. Box 347392
Parma, OH 44134
Telephone: (330) 722-1627
E-mail: birdrescue5@hotmail.com
www.birdrescue.com

Parrot Rehabilitation Society
P.O. Box 620213
San Diego, CA 92102
Telephone: (619) 224-6712
E-mail: prsorg@yahoo.com
www.parrotsociety.org

TARA
Tuscon Avian Rescue and Adoption
Foundation
P.O. Box 36984
Tucson, AZ 85704
Telephone: (520) 747-0554
E-mail: admin@tarafoundation.com
www.tarafoundation.com

Veterinary Resources

Association of Avian Veterinarians
P.O.Box 811720
Boca Raton, FL 33481-1720
Telephone: (561) 393-8901
Fax: (561) 393-8902
E-mail: AAVCTRLOFC@aol.com
www.aav.org

Internet Resources

BirdCLICK
www.geocities.com/Heartland/Acres/9154/
(a website about clicker training birds)

Holistic Bird
www.holisticbird.org

International Conure Association
www.conure.org

Living and Learning With Parrots
www.Behaviorworks.org

The Parrot Pages
www.parrotpages.com

World Parrot Trust
www.worldparrottrust.org

Books

Arndt, T. *Atlas of Conures, Aratingas and Pyrrhuras.* Neptune City, NJ: T.F.H. Publications, 1993

Deutsch, R. *The Healthy Bird Cookbook.* Neptune City, NJ: T.F.H. Publications, 2005.

Forshaw, J. M. and Frank Knight, *Parrots of the World.* Princeton: Princeton University Press, 2006

Gallerstein, Gary A., *The Complete Pet Bird Owner's Handbook.* Minneapolis, MN: Avian Publications, 2003.

Magazines

Bird Talk
3 Burroughs
Irvine, CA 92618
Telephone: 949-855-8822
Fax: (949) 855-3045
www.birdtalkmagazine.com

Bird Times
7-L Dundas Circle
Greensboro, NC 27407
Telephone: (336) 292-4247
Fax: (336) 292-4272
E-mail: info@petpublishing.com
www.birdtimes.com

Good Bird
PO Box 684394
Austin, TX 78768
Telephone: 512-423-7734
Fax: (512) 236-0531
E-mail: info@goodbirdinc.com
www.goodbirdinc.com

Parrots
Imax Ltd.
Riverside Business Centre
Brighton Road, Shore-by-Sea,
BN43 6RE
Telephone: 01273 464 777
E-Mail: info@imaxweb.co.uk
www.parrotmag.com

The Companion Parrot Quarterly
Laughing Parrot Gallery & Avian
Education Center
239 E. 4th Street
Loveland, CO 80537
Telephone: (970) 278-0233
E-mail: staff@companionparrot.com
www.companionparrot.com

Index

Index

111

Index

Acknowledgments

The author wishes to thank Diane Grindol; the International Conure Association (especially Brent Andrus, Lisa McManus, and Cheryl Burns); Greg Burkett, DVM, Dipl. ABVP-Avian; and the Clackamas County and Multnomah County Library Systems.

About the Author

Writer and educator Carol Frischmann holds a B.S. in Science Education from Duke University. She is the pet columnist for KGW.com, an NBC-affiliated television station, and for her own website ThisWildLife.com. Three parrots and a Doberman pinscher closely supervise Carol's work in her Portland, Oregon office

Photo Credits